Freeway

Workbook – Ausgabe Wirtschaft
Englisch für berufliche Schulen

von
Catherine Küpper
Wolfgang Rosenkranz (Hrsg.)
Graham Tucker

Ernst Klett Verlag
Stuttgart · Leipzig

Business communication

Exam course

Vocabulary revision

1 People

Use the words in the box to fill in suitable pairs in the table below.

female – aunt – wife – women – son – dad – gentleman – life – grandchildren – child

1.	grandparents	
2.	men	
3.	daughter	
4.	adult	
5.	mum	
6.	husband	
7.	lady	
8.	male	
9.	uncle	
10.	death	

2 Jobs

Match the jobs on the left with a suitable description on the right by filling in the correct letter.

1.	a cook		a)	cares for sick people
2.	a farmer		b)	repairs machines
3.	a postman		c)	serves food and drinks in a restaurant
4.	a nursery school teacher		d)	prepares meals
5.	a landlady		e)	cuts and sells meat in a shop
6.	a mechanic		f)	rents rooms to other people
7.	a waiter		g)	cultivates land and raises animals
8.	a butcher		h)	sells goods in a shop
9.	a shop assistant		i)	cares for young children
10.	a nurse		j)	collects and delivers mail

3 Work – Crossword

Fill in the corresponding English words.

ACROSS

2. Angestellte/r, Beschäftigte/r
3. Bewerber/in
5. Karriere
8. Bewerbung
10. Hersteller, Produzent
11. verdienen
15. Wirtschaft

DOWN

1. Wettbewerb
4. Fabrik
6. Abteilung
7. Unternehmen
9. werben
12. Werkzeug
13. Käufer/in
14. Arbeit(splatz), Beruf

4 The home, rooms and furniture

Give the names of the parts of the house (numbers 1 and 2), the rooms (numbers 3 to 6) and the pieces of furniture (numbers 7 to 18).
Use a separate sheet of paper.

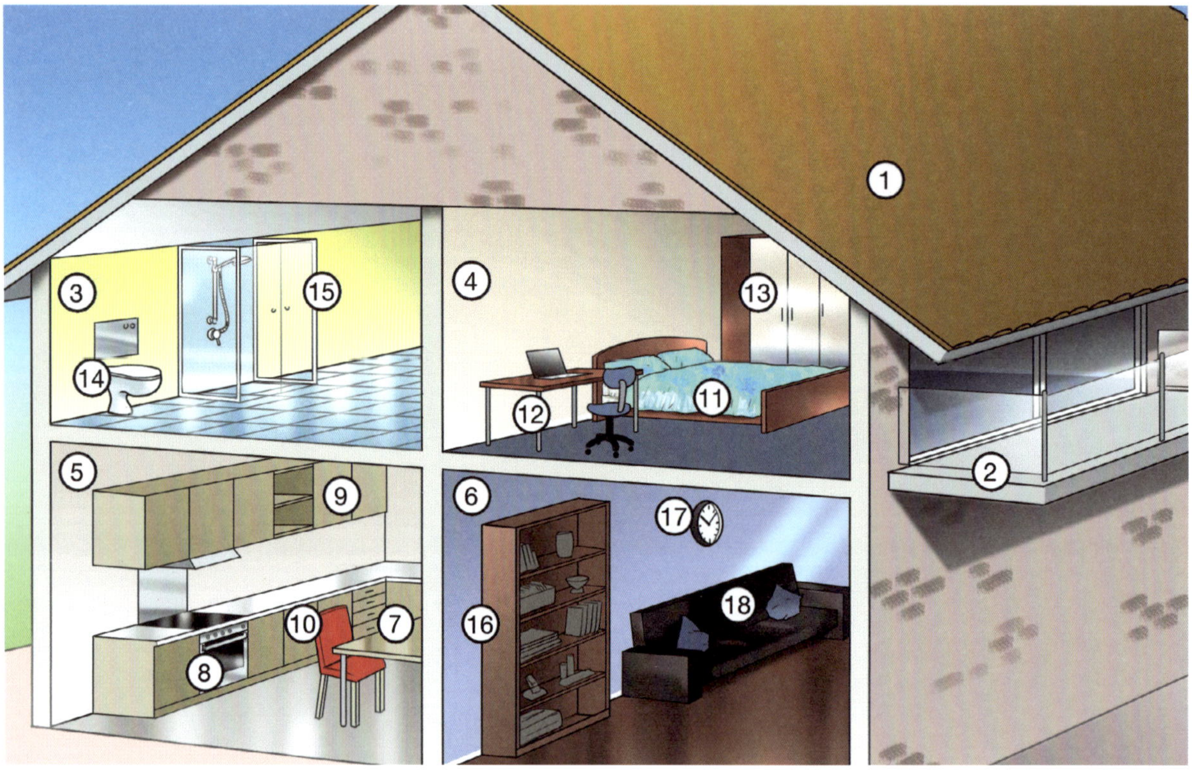

5 Traffic and transport

Use the endings in the box to create English words to do with traffic and transport. Then translate the words into German. If you are not sure, check the list of basic vocabulary in your student's book.

dent – ort – gage – cycle – ine – form – icle – ney – way – case – et –
ival – enger – toms – rol – go – ry – ght – eel – ver

	English word	German translation
1.	bi	
2.	airp	
3.	pass	
4.	acci	
5.	rail	
6.	plat	
7.	bag	
8.	car	
9.	veh	
10.	wh	

	English word	German translation
11.	dri	
12.	fli	
13.	eng	
14.	pet	
15.	tick	
16.	arr	
17.	suit	
18.	cus	
19.	jour	
20.	lor	

6 The body, clothes and accessories

Find words for the parts of the body, clothes and accessories.
Use a separate sheet of paper.

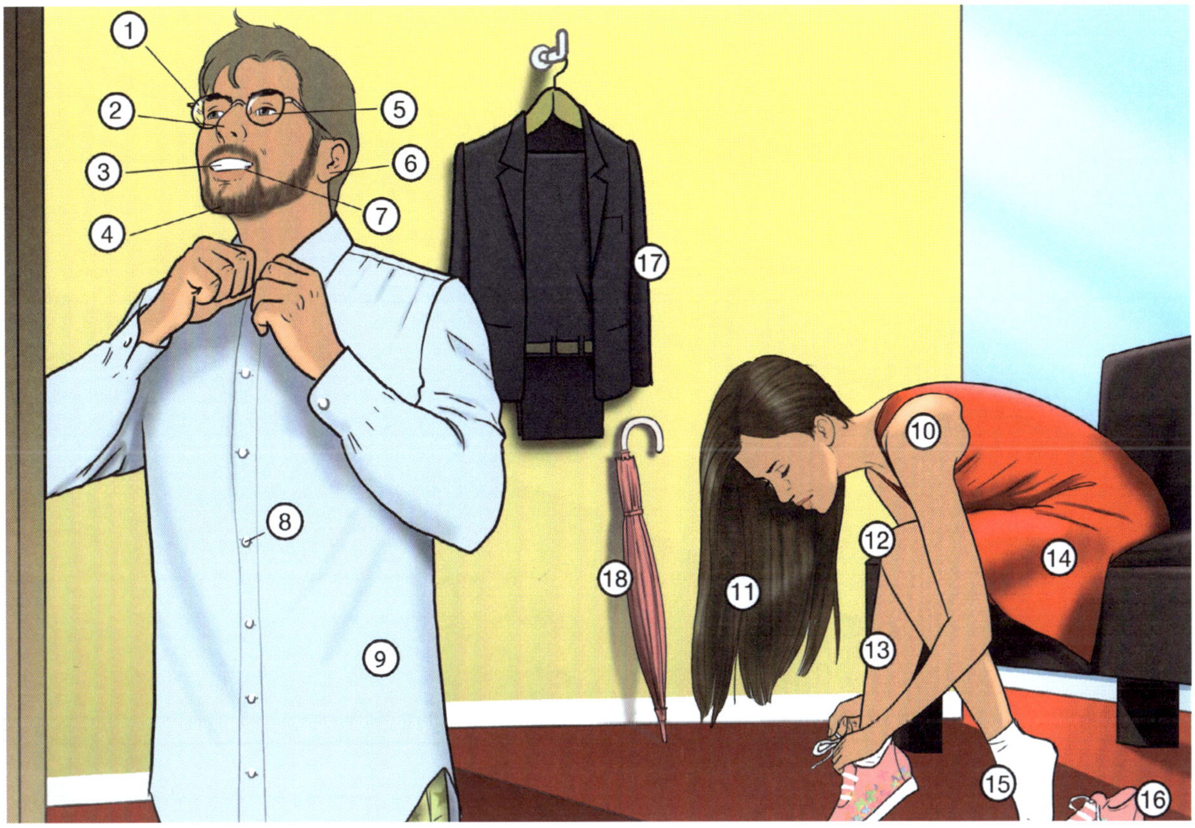

7 At school

Match the words in the table below with their definitions and fill in the correct letter.

1.	teacher		a)	a child in school
2.	pupil		b)	a place where classes meet
3.	class		c)	a dark surface in a classroom for writing
4.	classroom		d)	task that a student is given to do at home
5.	classmate		e)	a piece of furniture that is like a table and is used for writing
6.	desk		f)	a person whose job it is to instruct students
7.	lesson		g)	group of students who meet at school regularly
8.	blackboard		h)	a white stick used for writing in class
9.	a piece of chalk		i)	a member of the same class
10.	homework		j)	a period of time when people are taught
11.	attend		k)	give lessons
12.	teach		l)	regularly go to (school)

8 Eating and drinking

Fill in the missing vowels. Then fill in the German meanings of the words.

Example: l_m_n = lemon - Zitrone

1.	l_nch		**16.**	v_g_t_bl_	
2.	m_rm_l_d_		**17.**	w_n_	
3.	m_ _t		**18.**	_ppl_	
4.	m_lk		**19.**	b_ttl_	
5.	p_t_t_		**20.**	br_ _d	
6.	s_g_r		**21.**	br_ _kf_st	
7.	s_pp_r		**22.**	c_k_	
8.	d_nn_r		**23.**	ch_c_l_t_	
9.	t_ _		**24.**	ch_ _s_	
10.	t_m_t_		**25.**	ch_ps	
11.	c_ff_ _		**26.**	sp_ _n	
12.	c_p		**27.**	kn_f_	
13.	pl_t_		**28.**	_c_ cr_ _m	
14.	_gg		**29.**	sw_ _t	
15.	f_rk		**30.**	h_ngr_	

9 Using adjectives to describe people and things

Match the following German words in the list with their English equivalents in the box.

active – angry – beautiful – bored – boring – careful – careless – certain – clever – different – difficult – dirty – friendly – hungry – important – interesting – surprised – tired – unfriendly – unhappy

1.	interessant		**11.**	unfreundlich	
2.	langweilig		**12.**	gelangweilt	
3.	unterschiedlich, verschieden		**13.**	sicher, bestimmt, gewiss	
4.	müde		**14.**	überrascht	
5.	wütend		**15.**	vorsichtig, sorgfältig	
6.	freundlich		**16.**	sorglos	
7.	aktiv		**17.**	schwierig	
8.	schön		**18.**	unglücklich	
9.	schmutzig		**19.**	klug, schlau	
10.	hungrig		**20.**	wichtig	

10 What people do (verbs + prepositions and particles)

Complete the following sentences by filling in a suitable word from the box below.

about – after – down – for – for – from – off – on – on – on – over –
to – up – with

1. The student applied __________ a part-time job.
2. She was looking __________ a job where she could work late in the afternoon.
3. First the student enquired __________ the company.
4. She listened carefully __________ what a friend said.
5. The company deals __________ all sorts of goods.
6. Their success depends __________ the quality of the goods.
7. Their products differ __________ products made by other companies.
8. In her job the student has to look __________ the customers' children.
9. She often sits __________ with the children and reads stories to them.
10. When she turns __________ the page she asks the children how they think the story will go __________.
11. The children put __________ their hands when they have an interesting idea.
12. After the children have left the room the student turns __________ the lights, puts __________ her coat and goes home.

11 Nature – Crossword

Complete the following table by filling in the corresponding English words. Then you can read the solution from top to bottom.

1. Energie, Kraft
2. Pflanze
3. Fluss
4. Entfernung
5. Baum
6. Umweltverschmutzung
7. Dunkelheit
8. Atmosphäre
9. Meer
10. Sonnenschein
11. Wetter

Solution

1.														
2.														
3.														
4.														
5.														
6.														
7.														
8.														
9.														
10.														
11.														

Grammar revision

1 Articles

a) Fill in "a" or "an". ► Indefinite article, p. 211

1.	a	student	**5.**	an	examination
2.	an	exercise	**6.**	a	university
3.	an	address	**7.**	an	hour
4.	a	college	**8.**	a	office

b) Fill in "the" where necessary. ► Definite article article, p. 211

Visiting a friend in London

My English friend Derek goes to [1.] ______ college. When I visited him he showed me [2.] the ______ college buildings. Next year he will attend [3.] to the ______ university. Maybe he can study at [4.] the ______ University of Bournemouth. In my next holidays I will go to [5.] the ______ Great Britain. I will be in [6.] ______ London and will see [7.] The ______ Thames and [8.] the ______ Buckingham Palace. I would like to fly to [9.] the ______ London Gatwick Airport. I hope that my friend can meet me at [10.] the ______ airport.

2 Irregular plural forms

a) Complete the following list of singular and plural forms. Watch the spelling of the words!
► Plural, p. 212

	Singular	Plural		Singular	Plural
1.	man	men	**7.**	live	lives
2.	university	universities	**8.**	foot	foots
3.	address		**9.**		teeth
4.	woman	women	**10.**	yourself	yourselves
5.	city	cities	**11.**	copy	copys
6.	child	children	**12.**	wife	wifes

b) Write the words from the box below under the correct headings.
(Singular or Plural)

information – jeans – ~~weather~~ – ~~glasses (*Brille*)~~ – ~~homework~~ – furniture – trousers – knowledge – ~~mathematics~~ – news – work – nature – clothes – advice – economics – hair

Singular	
information	is
weather	
homework	

Plural	
jeans	are
mathematics	
glasses	

3 Some or any?

► Some or any? p. 216

Fill in "some" or "any".

At the market

Customer: I'd like [1.] some red apples, please.

Salesperson: Here you are. Is there [2.] anything else I can do for you?

Customer: Yes, I can't see [3.] ______ strawberries here. Have you got [4.] ______ ?

Salesperson: Of course. We've got [5.] ______ very sweet ones over here. Would you like [6.] ______ ?

Customer: Oh yes. I love strawberries. And I mustn't forget to get [7.] ______ bananas.

Salesperson: That's five pounds then.

Customer: Oh dear! I haven't got [8.] ______ small change. Can you change a twenty-pound note?

Salesperson: No problem. That's fine.

4 Much – many – (a) little – (a) few

► Much – many – a lot of, p. 217 ► Little / a little – few / a few, p. 217

Fill in the following gaps with "much, many, a lot of, little, a little, few, a few".

Travelling in winter

During the winter only [1.] a few people stay at seaside hotels in southern England. There is not [2.] ___ to do and so [3.] ___ people stay at home. If they have saved [4.] ___ money, young people book cheap flights to Majorca and spend [5.] ___ days there. It's just about a thousand miles away. After [6.] ___ hours they land in Majorca, where [7.] ___ of them enjoy parties and have [8.] ___ fun.

5 Prepositions

► Some important prepositions, p. 213

Fill in suitable prepositions from the box.

at – at – at – at – at – on – on – on – in – in – in – in – in – by – by – past – until – to – to

Arriving in London

When Melinda landed [1.] at London Gatwick Airport [2.] ___ a Saturday [3.] ___ June she arrived just [4.] ___ time for the Wimbledon tennis championships. She is very interested [5.] ___ sports and so she tried to get some tickets. First she went to the city centre [6.] ___ train and then she went [7.] ___ a ticket office [8.] ___ foot. When she arrived [9.] ___ five minutes [10.] ___ six, she found that the office had just closed [11.] ___ six o'clock. So she went to her hostel [12.] ___ bus. [13.] ___ the hostel she booked tickets [14.] ___ the Internet there. Later on [15.] ___ the evening she went [16.] ___ the cinema and watched the latest Leonardo di Caprio film. She came back to her hostel [17.] ___ midnight and slept [18.] ___ 9 o'clock [19.] ___ the morning.

6 Adjectives

a) **Write the forms of comparison of the adjectives in the box under the suitable heading.** ► Comparison of adjectives, p. 214

small – **beautiful** – **good** – **easy** – big – cheap – difficult – nice – heavy – tall – attractive – elegant – hungry – bad – much – intelligent – happy – hot – little – large – interesting – healthy

Adjective	-er	-est
small	smaller	smallest
easy	easier	easiest

Adjective	more	most
beautiful	more beautiful	most beautiful

Adjective	irregular *(unregelmäßig)*	irregular *(unregelmäßig)*
good	better	best

b) **Study the following example and compare the phones and the buildings below.**

Example:
1. **Mobile phone 2 is cheaper than mobile phone 3.**
2. **Mobile phone 2 is not as cheap as phone 1.**
3. **Mobile phone 1 is the cheapest.**

Empire State Building (381 m), USA

Shanghai Tower (632 m), China

Burj Khalifa (828 m), Dubai

1. Mobile phone 3 is more expensive than ______________________
2. Mobile phone 1 is ______________________
3. Mobile phone 3 is ______________________

____

____

____

____

____

____

7 Question tags

a) **Complete the sentences with suitable question tags from the box.** ► Question tags, p. 224

aren't you – isn't she – don't you – don't they – haven't they – won't they – won't you – is she – have they – aren't they

Meeting a person and asking questions in a polite way

1. You are from Boston, aren't you ?
2. You live in Liverpool, don't you ?
3. Your friend Tracy isn't from Boston, is she ?
4. Tracy is from England, ______________?
5. Tracy and Sharon are staying in Paris at the moment, ______________?
6. They love France, ______________?
7. They have been to France several times, ______________?
8. But they haven't seen the Port of Marseille yet, ______________?
9. They will come back next week, ______________?
10. You will meet them at the airport, ______________?

b) **Complete the following sentences with suitable question tags on your own.**

The development of our planet

1. Many people are worried about our nature, ______________________________?
2. They do not believe in a positive development, ______________________________?
3. The earth is getting warmer, ______________________________?
4. We are consuming too much water, ______________________________?
5. We haven't paid enough attention to our environment, ______________________________?
6. Last year, people bought more cars than in the years before, ______________________________?
7. We can all do something, ______________________________?
8. You will come to our meeting tomorrow, ______________________________?

8 Possessive case – Whose?

► Possessive case, p. 213

Fill in the missing word.

1. This book belongs to Jerry. It is Jerry's book.
2. Only girls go to this school. It is a girls' school.
3. This laptop belongs to my parents. It is my ______________ laptop.
4. The Smiths own this house. This is the ______________ house.
5. The children are playing with their toys. These are the ______________ toys.
6. This secretary works for the Prime Minister. She is the ______________ secretary.
7. Those people have to look after patients at a hospital. Caring for patients is those ______________ duty.
8. I bought this newspaper yesterday. It is ______________ newspaper.

9 Word order

► Word order with adverbs and adverbials, p. 216

Put the following parts of the sentences in the right order.

Christmas shopping

1. a lot of people and cars / in the streets / there are
   There are a lot of people and cars in the streets.
2. quickly / walking / to the bus stop / are / some people
   ____
3. at the red lights / the cars / waiting / at the moment / are
   ____
4. crossing / some shoppers / the street / in a hurry / are
   ____
5. lots of presents / they / bought / in the department stores / have / already
   ____
6. to their children / these presents / on Christmas Day / they / want to give
   ____

Unit 1

Young people in the world of work

A | Getting started: First steps into the world of work

1 Young people's posts ► Vokabeln systematisch lernen, S. 261

Find the words and phrases in the texts which match the following definitions.

Post Emma (→ page 8)

1.	training for a few weeks or months (often not paid) in order to get work experience	
2.	understanding of a new situation or a new job	
3.	in a foreign country	
4.	make arrangements at hotel reception when you arrive and want to stay there	

Post Tom (→ page 9)

5.	a shop for customers who make or repair things themselves	
6.	parts of a city that are furthest away from the centre	
7.	flat boards on which products are stored in a shop	

Post Zuzanna (→ page 18)

8.	a person who helps other employees in an office	
9.	important parts of a company	
10.	something you do in a regular way	

B | Grammar

2 Introducing a person ► Present simple, p. 219

Complete the following text about Tracy using the verbs in the box.

be – have (2×) – love – play – drive – come – live – work – chat

Hi! I would like to introduce my friend Tracy. She [1.] ____________ seventeen years old and she [2.] ____________ from England. She [3.] ____________ a brother and a sister. They [4.] ____________ in a flat in Liverpool. Tracy's mother [5.] ____________ as a nurse and her father [6.] ____________ a bus. Tracy [7.] ____________ a part-time job in a fast food restaurant. In her free time she [8.] ____________ with friends on the Internet or [9.] ____________ volleyball. She [10.] ____________ her cats 'Trisha' and 'Trix'.

3 At college
► Present simple, p. 219

Ask and answer questions using the prompts given.

1. enjoy languages? (yes) Do you enjoy languages? – Yes, I do.
2. like maths? (no) Do you like maths? – No, I don't.
3. be interested in sports? (yes) Are you interested in sports? – Yes, I am.
4. eat lunch at college? (yes) ______
5. prefer IT to Business Studies? (no) ______
6. start college at half past nine? (no) ______
7. go home by bus? (yes) ______
8. take tests in every subject? (yes) ______
9. have exams? (yes) ______
10. be nervous before exams? (yes) ______

4 What are they doing?
► Present continuous, p. 220

Say what the following persons are doing and what they are not doing.

1. **Example: Will – cycle?** Is Will cycling? – No, Will is not cycling, he is driving a car.
2. **Example: Sue and Ellen – send text messages?** Are Sue and Ellen sending text messages? – No, they are not sending text messages, they are talking on the phone.
3. Marco – sleep? ______
4. Lisa and Sam – talk? ______
5. Sarah – work? ______

6. Sabrina – watch TV? ______

7. Julio – sing? ______

8. The girls – play volleyball? ______

5 After college ► Present simple, p. 219 ► Present continuous, p. 220

a) Complete the following list of tense markers with the words from the box.

> **now** – **normally** – this afternoon – today – every weekend – at the moment – right now – every Monday – on Sundays – usually – regularly

Tense markers

Present simple	Present continuous
normally	now

b) Complete the following text. Watch out for the correct tenses.

After college Lucy and Stan normally **[1. work]** work part-time at *Macy's Superstore* but they **[2. not work]** are not working there now. Stan is sick and **[3. stay]** ______ home this afternoon. Usually Stan **[4. go]** ______ to the store by bike but right now his sister Anna **[5. use]** ______ it because she has to do the shopping today. **[6. want]** ______ she ______ to go shopping? No, Anna **[7. not like]** ______ shopping. Anna's friend Lucy **[8. take]** ______ part in a sports competition with another college today. Every Monday she **[9. train]** ______ at college with some other girls from her course and they regularly **[10. meet]** ______ at a friend's house and **[11. practise]** ______ for more than three hours. At the moment Lucy and her friends **[12. stand]** ______ in front of the gym and **[13. wait]** ______ for the beginning of the competition.

6 Managing situations ► Present simple, p. 219 ► Present continuous, p. 220

M

a) Sagen Sie einem englischsprachigen Gast, …

1. dass Sie das Kolleg besuchen. ______
2. welche Fächer Sie mögen bzw. nicht mögen. ______
3. ob Sie am Nachmittag / Abend / Wochenende arbeiten. ______
4. was Sie zurzeit tun. ______

b) **Fragen Sie Ihren Gast, …**

1. woher er / sie kommt. ____________________
2. wie lange er / sie bleibt. ____________________
3. wie ihm / ihr Ihr Ort gefällt. ____________________
4. ob er / sie Deutsch spricht. ____________________

C | Reading: Living and working in London

7 Let's share the flat! – Verbs and nouns → page 12

Complete the following list of words from the text with suitable verbs or nouns.

	Verb	Noun
1.	to decide	
2.	to communicate	
3.		placement
4.		checkout
5.	to improve	
6.	to share	
7.		life
8.		trouble
9.	to guess	
10.	to sound	

8 Let's share the flat! – Antonyms → page 12

Find the opposites (antonyms) of the following words and phrases in the text.

1.	decreasing	
2.	to stay in one's home country	
3.	to keep all of it for oneself	
4.	worse	
5.	boring	
6.	packing	

7.	unfortunately	
8.	badly	
9.	the same	
10.	from one's own country	
11.	to make worse	
12.	together	

D | Practice

9 Training skills – How to describe pictures

► Fotos und Illustrationen beschreiben / analysieren, S. 243

a) Complete the following description of the photo by filling in verbs from the box below and the phrases given in the picture.

concentrate – hold – lean – prepare – seem – **show** – stand – train – try – use – want – wear

The colour photo [1.] shows a scene in a restaurant kitchen. Three people [2.] ____________ in front of a stove in the [3.] ____________. On the [4.] ____________ we can see a young woman who [5.] ____________ a pan. In the [6.] ____________ a young man [7.] ____________ a ladle to show soup to an older man on the [8.] ____________ who [9.] ____________ forward in order to have a better look. The two younger people [10.] ____________ white working clothes while the older person has a dark shirt on. He [11.] ____________ to be the head chef. Perhaps he [12.] ____________ to taste the soup. In the [13.] ____________ on the left we can see another young person who [14.] ____________ meals. All the people are busy and [15.] ____________ on their work. Maybe all these young people [16.] ____________ to become chefs and [17.] ____________ to do their very best.

P **b) Describe and analyze the following photo in a similar way. The words in the box may help you.**

to hike – countryside – backpack – hiking stick – map – walking-tour – hiker

10 Jobs – Crossword

Fill in the following crossword puzzle with suitable English words from pages 14 and 15 of your student's book.

ACROSS

1. Tourismus
4. Beruf, Beschäftigung
6. sparen
7. Steuer
8. Vordergrund
11. Verkaufsraum
13. beraten
14. Büro

DOWN

2. unterstützen
3. Hintergrund
5. Werbung
9. Großhandel
10. Praxis
12. Lohn, Gehalt

E | Reading +

11 Work on a farm – and see the world for free → page 16

Complete the summary using suitable words from the text.

If you are interested in travelling the world but you cannot afford it, a "Work and [1.] Travel" programme may be for you. There are many projects in Australia and New Zealand which offer free [2.] ________ and [3.] ________ to people who are prepared to work on [4.] ________. The [5.] ________ of your stay is flexible. You can stay for a few weeks or for [6.] ________ months. This must be [7.] ________ with the farm owners. You can learn or do many different things but before accepting an offer [8.] ________ carefully what is [9.] ________ of you. Eight hours of [10.] ________ labour can be hard for an untrained person. If you are not sure about your [11.] ________ so far from home, you should travel with a friend. Before deciding look on the Internet for [12.] ________ from former travellers. The *WWOOF* groups offer a [13.] ________ of hosts. First you have to join one of the groups which can cost you up to [14.] ________.

Unit 2

Getting a job

A | Getting started: Big companies

1 A name behind many names → page 21 ► Vokabeln systematisch lernen, S. 261

Find synonyms for the following words in the text. Fill in the suitable form of the word and the line where you have found it.

	Word	Synonym in the text	Line
1.	to establish		
2.	to put a product on the market		
3.	highly		
4.	famous		
5.	to rise		
6.	goods		
7.	in the meantime		
8.	to buy		
9.	to concentrate		

2 International markets ► Vokabeln systematisch lernen, S. 261

Complete the following list of geographical regions with countries from the box below (four countries per region).

Korea – Chile – Lebanon – Namibia – Bolivia – Cameroon – Japan – Nigeria – Iran – Iraq – Argentina – Saudi Arabia – Brazil – Vietnam – Indonesia – Angola

1.	Latin America	
2.	Africa	
3.	the Middle East	
4.	Asia	

B | Grammar

3 The development of a company
► Past simple, p. 221

a) Complete the following text about *The Times* by using the right forms of the verbs in the simple past.

John Walter __was__ the first editor of *The Times* newspaper in 1785. He __called__ it *The Daily Universal Register* at that time but it __did not become__ popular under this name. So Walter **[1. change]** ____________ the title to *The Times* three years later. In 1803 he **[2. hand]** ____________ the newspaper over to his son. At that time the profits of *The Times* **[3. be]** ____________ high because there **[4. not be]** ____________ many other newspapers on the market. Walter **[5. have]** ____________ very good writers because he **[6. pay]** ____________ them very well. The influence of *The Times* **[7. rise]** ____________ even more by the beginning of the 19th century. The newspaper was the first that **[8. send]** ____________ war correspondents to write about conflicts in other countries. Different people **[9. own]** ____________ *The Times* in the following years. It **[10. not be]** ____________ until 1966 that *The Times* **[11. print]** ____________ news on its front page, previously it only **[12. publish]** ____________ small advertisements there. In 1981 the Australian Rupert Murdoch **[13. buy]** ____________ *The Times* and **[14. introduce]** ____________ new computer technology.

b) Make questions about the following words taken from the text above.

1. *The Daily Universal Register* __What did John Walter call the newspaper first?__
2. three years later
   ____
3. because there were not many other newspapers on the market
   ____
4. very well
   ____
5. war correspondents
   ____
6. news
   ____
7. new computer technology
   ____

4 Preparing for an interview

► Past simple, p. 221 ► Present perfect simple, p. 222

a) **Greg Wilson has a job interview tomorrow. He has made some notes in order to prepare for the interview. Underline the time expressions in the notes and decide which tense you must use with these time expressions.**

b) **Make complete sentences about Greg in the correct tense.**

Examples:

1. born in 1998 (simple past) Greg was born in 1998.
2. school until 2014 (simple past) He went to school until 2014.
3. interested in computers for a long time now (present perfect simple)
   He has been interested in computers for a long time now.
4. live / in Liverpool / from 1998 to 2002 (______)
   ______
5. family / move / to Birmingham / in 2002 (______)
   ______
6. live / in Birmingham / since then (______)
   ______
7. join / a computer club / four years ago (______)
   ______
8. pass / exams / in 2014 (______)
   ______
9. find / a good job training programme / after his exams (______)
   ______
10. be / with that company / for a few years now (______)
   ______

5 For or since?

► Present perfect simple, p. 222 ► Present perfect continuous, p. 223

Re-write the following sentences by replacing "since" or "for" and by changing the time expression.

Example: It's Monday now. Simon hasn't seen Jane since Friday.

Simon hasn't seen Jane for three days.

1. It's October 15 now. Sally has been ill for two weeks.
   Sally has been ill since …
2. It's the end of August now. It hasn't rained in Cornwall for a month now.
   ______
3. It's Friday evening now. The manager has been in China since Monday morning.
   ______
4. It's Christmas now. Sarah hasn't had a big party since last Christmas.
   ______
5. It's half past ten now. Nick has been watching TV for four hours now.
   ______

6 A job interview

► Past simple, p. 221 ► Present perfect simple, p. 222

Complete the following job interview between Judy Hill and Susan Sunday by filling in the right forms of the verbs in the past simple or present perfect simple.

Judy: Hello there, Susan. First of all, can you tell me something about yourself?

Susan: I **[1. be born]** ____________ in York on 2nd September 2000. I **[2. live]** ____________ there for four years. Then we all **[3. move]** ____________ to Swindon because my father **[4. find]** ____________ a better job there.

Judy: **[5. go]** ____________ you ____________ to school in Swindon then?

Susan: Yes, I **[6. do]** ____________ ! I **[7. attend]** ____________ school there until 2016.

Judy: I see from your application that you **[8. be]** ____________ interested in designing clothes for a long time. At what age **[9. start]** ____________ you ____________ that?

Susan: It all **[10. begin]** ____________ when I **[11. spend]** ____________ a holiday with my aunt about six or seven years ago. She not only **[12. teach]** ____________ me to design clothes but also how to make my own dresses. So in the last few years I **[13. make]** ____________ quite a lot of clothes – not only for myself but also for friends.

Judy: **[14. do]** ____________ you already ____________ a placement in that field?

Susan: I **[15. not do]** ____________ a placement yet but I **[16. take]** ____________ some courses at college in the past few months. And in my last summer holidays I **[17. help]** ____________ my aunt in her clothes shop. I **[18. enjoy]** ____________ that very much. That's one reason why I **[19. apply]** ____________ to your company.

7 Managing situations

M

► Past simple, p. 221 ► Present perfect simple, p. 222

Sie haben sich bei einem internationalen Unternehmen um einen Ausbildungsplatz beworben. Ein Teil Ihres Bewerbungsgesprächs findet deshalb auf Englisch statt. Sagen Sie dem Interviewer / der Interviewerin, dass Sie . . .

1. schon viel über das Unternehmen gehört haben.

   ____

2. sich im Internet über das Unternehmen informiert haben.

   ____

3. erst vor einem Jahr hierher gezogen sind.

   ____

4. bereits ein Praktikum absolviert haben.

   ____

5. schon immer für ein internationales Unternehmen arbeiten wollten.

   ____

C | Reading: Applications

8 Applications → page 24 / 25

Match the phrases on the left with suitable phrases on the right to make meaningful sentences according to the documents in your student's book.

1.		Julia is a student	a)	basic computer skills.
2.		She would like to apply	b)	to going to the interview at a company.
3.		Julia is interested	c)	of French and Spanish.
4.		She has experience	d)	for a work placement in London.
5.		The young woman has a good working knowledge	e)	for a person who is able to work in a team.
6.		The company is looking	f)	in working at a big company.
7.		The company needs a person who has	g)	in working part-time at a local store.
8.		The applicant is looking forward	h)	at a college of further education.

D | Practice

9 Finding the right candidate → page 26 ► Vokabeln systematisch lernen, S. 261

Fill in the jobs that young people can learn at these workplaces.

1.	shop	
2.	travel agency	
3.	tax consultant office	
4.	doctor's practice	
5.	bank	
6.	advertising agency	
7.	import company	
8.	car salesroom	

10 A placement on offer

Complete the following text about two students by filling in "ed" or "ing".

1. Julia is interest__________ in finding a work placement in Britain.
2. She is really motivat__________ and has already written several applications.
3. She hopes that a placement abroad could be very interest__________.
4. When she receives some answers from British companies she gets excit__________.
5. Of course, positive reactions to her applications are motivat__________.
6. One offer seems excit__________. Julia could do a placement in a big company on the Isle of Wight!

E | Reading +

11 Training skills – How to describe statistics

► Diagramme beschreiben / analysieren, S. 245

a) Match the names of the graphs in the box with the pictures.

pie chart – line graph – bar chart

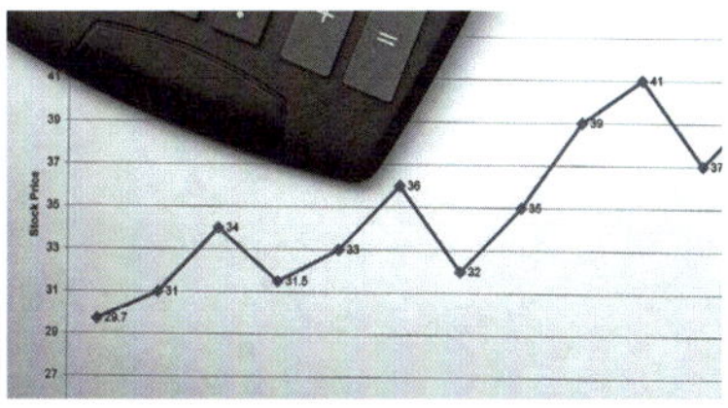

1. ______________________

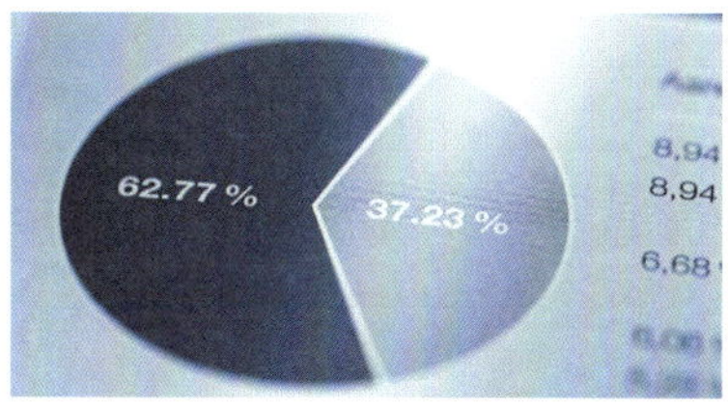

2. ______________________

3. ______________________

b) Read the description of the following pie chart, complete the last sentence and fill in the data in the chart.

This pie chart shows the different age groups at YOUR HOST INTERNATIONAL. 10 per cent of the staff are younger than 20. The percentage of those between 30 and 39 amounts to 25 per cent. 18 per cent of YHO's staff are between 40 and 49. The most important group is the 20-to-29-year olds at about 40 per cent.

Only [1.] ______________ per cent of the employees are [2.] ______________ years or older.

The different age groups at YOUR HOST INTERNATIONAL

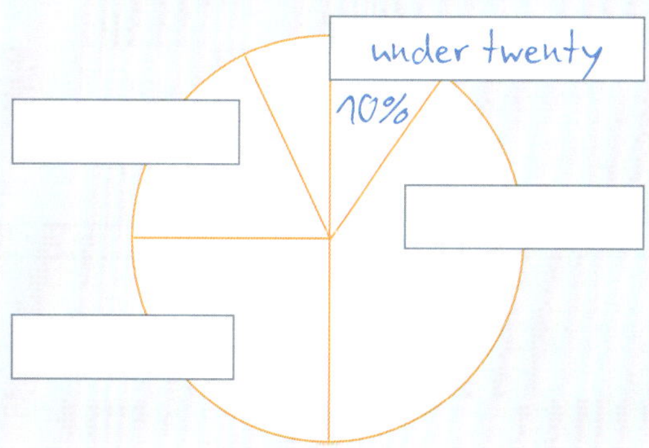

c) Complete the description of the bar chart below.

Number of applicants at YOUR HOST INTERNATIONAL

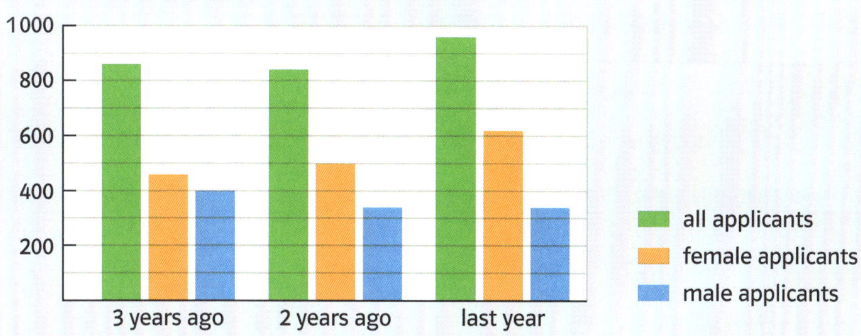

This [1.] ______________________ chart shows the development of the number of [2.] ______________________ for a job at YOUR HOST INTERNATIONAL: Three years ago the number totalled 860 with [3.] ______________________ women and 400 men. In the following year the number of applicants [4.] ______________________ slightly to 840 although the number of women significantly [5.] ______________________ by 40. So the number of male applicants fell sharply by [6.] ______________________ per cent. Last year the total number grew [7.] ______________________ to 960. The number of male applicants [8.] ______________________ at the same level while the number of female applicants [9.] ______________________ again.

Unit A

Preparing for a work placement in London

1 England, Britain or the UK?

a) Fill in the names of the countries and their capitals as shown on the map.

1.		a)	
2.		b)	
3.		c)	
4.		d)	
5.		e)	

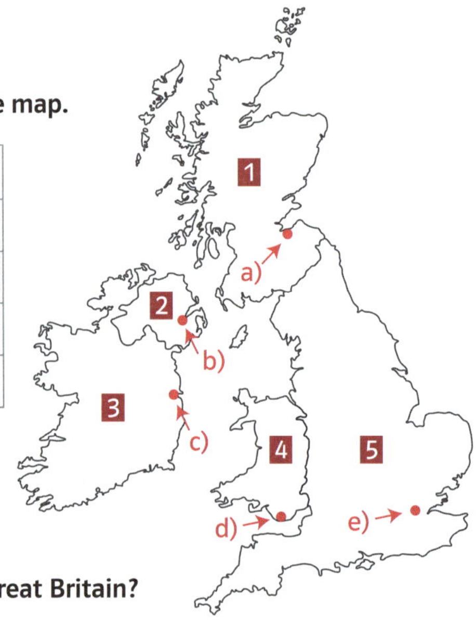

b) Which of the countries does not belong to the United Kingdom?

____

c) Which of the countries belongs to the United Kingdom but not to Great Britain?

____

d) Which of the capitals is not only the capital of one country but also the capital of the United Kingdom?

____

2 Writing an e-mail

Jenny Lucas has received an offer of a placement with a big British newspaper. Complete her e-mail by using words from the box. Remember to begin some words with a capital letter.

forward – getting to know – placement – dear – thank you very much – yours sincerely – as you know – experience – glad – working

[1.] __________ Mr Lovell

[2.] __________ for your offer. I am very [3.] __________ that you are giving me the chance of [4.] __________ the production of a big newspaper from the inside. [5.] __________ I am doing a [6.] __________ at our local newspaper but working at your company will be a great [7.] __________ for me.

I look [8.] __________ to [9.] __________ with you.

[10.] __________

Jenny Lucas

3 Making a phone call

a) Choose suitable words from the box and fill them in.

check – sorry – reduction – lot – vacancies – help – is – offer – far – spell – moment

1. Can I ________________ you?
2. Do you have any ________________?
3. Just a ________________, please.
4. Let me ________________ this for you.
5. How much ________________ the room, please?
6. How ________________ is your hotel from the station?
7. I'm ________________. We don't ________________ lunch.
8. I can give you a ________________ of 10 per cent.
9. Could you ________________ your name for me, please?
10. Thanks a ________________.

b) Put the following parts of a telephone conversation in the right order. Write the corresponding numbers before the sentences.

		Receptionist
	A	Let me just check. – That would be alright for two weeks.
1	B	Hello. This is Edinburgh 3029483. Clare Duncan speaking. How can I help you?
	C	Thank you very much, Ms Lucas. We look forward to welcoming you on the tenth then.
	D	Do you need a single room or a double room?
	E	That will be £40.
	F	And when exactly would you arrive, Ms Lucas?
	G	I'm sorry. Breakfast is £10 extra.
	H	Would you just give me your name again, please, and your credit card details?

		Caller
	I	A single room, please.
	J	That's OK. Is breakfast included in the price?
	K	Fine. How much is the room, please?
2	L	Hello. My name's Jenny Lucas. I'm looking for a room for two weeks.
	M	On the tenth of next month. Do you have any vacancies then?
	N	So that's £50 per night then. I'll take it. How can I make a booking?
	O	Well, my name is Jenny Lucas – J-e-n-n-y-L-u-c-a-s. And I've got a SmartCard No. 2432 5436 7654 6789.
	P	Thank you for your help, bye-bye.

Unit 3

The youth market

A | Getting started: Young people as consumers

1 Young consumers hold the key to change

► Vokabeln systematisch lernen, S. 261

Match the following words and phrases with suitable definitions by filling in the right letter.

1.		to give a product an environmentally-friendly image	a)	brand
2.		a group of products that are all made by one company and all have the same name	b)	principle
3.		a rule or belief which helps you to decide what is right or wrong	c)	figures
4.		to make less confident or less hopeful	d)	to confuse
5.		to make someone uncertain or unable to understand something; to make something difficult to understand	e)	to greenwash
6.		to give a product the image of being produced in humane working conditions	f)	to discourage
7.		numbers which show an amount (e.g. of money)	g)	label
8.		the name of a clothing manufacturer or fashion designer	h)	to fairwash

B | Grammar

2 Shop till your drop

► Past simple, p. 221 ► Past perfect simple, p. 223

Describe Julia's shopping trip in complete sentences as in the examples.

Example 1:
10:20 leaves home / 10:30 takes the bus to the shopping centre

After Julia had left home she took the bus to the shopping centre.

Example 2:
10:50 drinks a cup of coffee / 10:45 (!) arrives at the shopping centre

Julia drank a cup of coffee after she had arrived at the shopping centre.

1. 11:00 enters the chemist's / 11:10 buys a bottle of shampoo

2. 11:30 tries on some trainers / 11:20 looks at new fitness equipment

3. 11:50 meets her friend Jenny / 12:00 have lunch together

4. 12:30 Jenny leaves / 12:45 Julia continues with her shopping

5. 13:15 goes to a clothes shop / 13:00 buys a magazine

6. 14:15 tries on some new clothes for an hour / 14:20 decides to go to the supermarket

7. 14:40 goes to the cash desk / 14:30 puts milk, bread and meat into her shopping basket

8. 14:50 leaves the shopping centre / 15:00 takes the bus home

3 A car crash on the way home ► Past simple, p. 221 ► Past continuous, p. 221

When Julia was coming home from the shops a few days ago, she saw a car crash and called the police. Afterwards she had to answer the following questions.

Example 1:

Police officer: Julia, what were you doing when you saw the crash? **[cross the street]**

Julia: I was crossing the street.

Example 2:

Police officer: Julia, what did you do then? **[call the ambulance and the police]**

Julia: I called the ambulance and the police.

1. Police officer: Where was the car coming from? **[petrol station]**

   Julia:

2. Police officer: What was the driver doing? **[use / mobile phone]**

   Julia:

3. Police officer: Why did his car hit the school bus? **[not watch / the traffic]**
   Julia: ______________________________

4. Police officer: What was the school bus driver doing? **[talk / to a pupil on the bus]**
   Julia: ______________________________

5. Police officer: What happened to the two vehicles? **[crash / in the middle of the street]**
   Julia: ______________________________

6. Police officer: What did you do after you had phoned us? **[get on / the school bus]**
   Julia: ______________________________

7. Police officer: What were the pupils doing when you entered the bus? **[cry]**
   Julia: ______________________________

4 Home at last

► Past simple, p. 221 ► Past continuous, p. 221

Use "while" or "when" to describe what happened or what was happening when Julia finally got home.

1. unpack / her bags – telephone / ring
   While/When Julia was unpacking her bags the telephone rang.
2. count / her money – drop / some coins
   ____
3. put / the food in the fridge – neighbour / knock / on the door
   ____
4. talk / to the neighbour – cat / run out
   ____
5. look for / cat – another accident / happen
   ____

Now go on. Make two more sentences in the same way.

____

____

5 The successful introduction of a new product

► The tenses, p. 219 – 223

Fill in the suitable tense to complete the following text.

When the *2W* advertising agency **[1. get]** got the chance to develop the advertising campaign for the new "CrispChoc" six months ago they **[2. be]** were very happy because it **[3. be]** had been hard work to persuade the biscuits producers. While they **[4. work]** ____________ on the project they **[5. have]** ____________ to work long hours, even at the weekends. But after they **[6. find]** ____________ the suitable key words *2W* **[7. invent]** ____________ a slogan which **[8. become]** ____________ really successful in the past few months. In the meantime the biscuit company **[9. sell]** ____________ millions of boxes of "CrispChoc". Of course, *2W* **[10. work]** ____________ on a new project now.

C | Reading

6 Buyers' training at schools → page 40/41

a) Find suitable synonyms or antonyms in the text and fill them in the following tables.

	Find a synonym for this word or phrase	Word or phrase in the text
1.	a few	
2.	require	
3.	to start, to launch	
4.	very important	
5.	80 %	
6.	up-to-date	
7.	to try hard	
8.	convinced	
9.	use money to pay	
10.	reasonable, wise to do	

	Find an antonym for this word or phrase	Word or phrase in the text
1.	difficult	
2.	oldest, out of fashion	
3.	high	
4.	off-line	
5.	more	
6.	to spend	
7.	minor	
8.	to reject, to refuse	
9.	most expensive	
10.	carelessly	

b) Complete the following text with suitable words from the tables above.

Many young people are [1.] ________________ in debt because they [2.] ________________ more money than they really have. For example they buy the [3.] ________________ mobile phone because they are [4.] ________________ that this is cool and will show that they are [5.] ________________.
Now, schools have [6.] ________________ a new programme which will help young people to manage their money. There young people learn that it is [7.] ________________ to plan future expenses and first to [8.] ________________ money so that they can then afford [9.] ________________ purchases. So next time you go [10.] ________________ ask yourself if you really [11.] ________________ the product or service and if you have the money before you click the "Buy" button.

7 Managing situations – Helping customers ► The tenses, p. 219 – 223

M

Sie bedienen einen englischsprachigen Kunden in einem Fotofachgeschäft. Sie fragen den Kunden, ...

1. wie Sie ihm helfen können.
2. wo er die Anzeige für die Digitalkamera gesehen hat.
3. ob er die Digitalkamera schon ausprobiert hat.
4. wie er sich gefühlt hat, als er die Digitalkamera ausprobiert hat.
5. ob er seine alte Digitalkamera noch mochte, nachdem er die neue ausprobiert hatte.

Bitte schreiben Sie die Fragen in Ihr Heft.

1. How can I help you?

8 Training skills – How to do a role play → page 41

a) **Put the following parts of a sales talk in the right order.**

	Sales assistant
	This netbook has a 10-inch screen and it's not expensive.
	No problem, sir. This here is our latest netbook. Would you be interested in learning some more about it?
1	Good morning, sir, how can I help you?
	We have a special offer today. It's only $199.
	Of course, sir. We have a wide range of laptops. What are you especially interested in?
	Thank you very much.
	No problem. The white one is the same price.
	You're welcome.

	Customer
	That would be nice.
	Well, I'd like to have a small one which I can put in my briefcase.
	How much is this model?
	That's fine. I'll take it.
2	Good morning. I'm interested in laptops. Have you got any special offers?
	And what about different colours? I'd prefer a white one.
	Thank you for your help.

b) **Find phrases in the dialogue above (8 a) which have a similar meaning to the following.**

1. How much does this laptop cost? How much is this model?
2. Would you like to have some more information about it? ______
3. That would be fine. ______
4. Do you offer different colours? ______
5. Thanks a lot for your assistance. ______
6. I'd like to have it. ______
7. I'd like a white laptop better. ______
8. Certainly, sir. ______
9. What can I do for you? ______
10. It only costs … ______
11. My pleasure. ______
12. No worries, sir. ______

P c) **Now play or re-write the dialogue (8 a). Change as many phrases as possible.**

D | Practice

9 Advertising – Crossword

Complete the crossword on the right with words from pages 42 and 43 of your student's book and find the solution.

1. fairer Handel (zwei Wörter)
2. Verlangen, Wunsch
3. Kurzform für Werbeanzeige
4. Kunde, Kundin
5. (Verkaufs-)Förderung
6. Aufmerksamkeit
7. Preis
8. Interesse
9. Medien
10. umgehen mit
11. erkennen, anerkennen
12. Markteinführung
13. Zielgruppe (zwei Wörter)
14. Werbesendung, Spot
15. Vorteil
16. Handeln, Aktion
17. Unternehmen

							Solution ▼								
1.															
2.															
3.															
4.															
5.															
6.															
7.															
8.															
9.															
10.															
11.															
12.															
13.															
14.															
15.															
16.															
17.															

E | Reading +: New trends in advertising

10 Digital advertising on the move

Fill in the missing words of the following word families.

	Verb	Noun	Adjective
1.	to interest		
2.		effect	
3.			informative
4.	to differ		
5.		reliance, reliability	
6.			special
7.	to regulate		
8.		creator, creation	
9.			live, alive
10.	to succeed		
11.		use, user	
12.			integrative

Unit 4

Media in our lives

A | Getting started

1 Watching TV → page 49 ► Vokabeln systematisch lernen, S. 261

With the help of the syllables in the box below write down ten words which appear in the text. The first syllable of each word has already been given. Each line represents a syllable.

a – ca – cade – cant – di – ence – ence – er – er – fer – fi – it – ment – mu – ni – ni – tain – ter – ti – tion – tions – tude

1. view___
2. de___
3. sig___ ___ ___
4. at___ ___
5. dif___ ___
6. au___ ___
7. gen___ ___ ___
8. en___ ___ ___
9. hab___
10. com___ ___ ___ ___

B | Grammar

2 Can you help me? – At the internet café ► Will-future, p. 224

Write the staff member's polite offers in complete sentences.

Example:
Customer: **I'd like to have a coffee, please.**
Staff member: **[serve / in a minute]** I'll serve it in a minute.

1. Customer: I don't know how to access the Internet.
   Staff: **[help / you]** ______________________________
   ____
2. Customer: There is no mouse here.
   Staff: **[bring / you / one]** ______________________________
3. Customer: What's the Internet address of the nearest hostel, please?
   Staff: **[look it up / for you]** ______________________________
4. Customer: How can I print this out?
   Staff: **[do it / for you]** ______________________________
5. Customer: I'd like to make an Internet phone call, please.
   Staff: **[show / you]** ______________________________
6. Customer: I'd like to pay, please.
   Staff: **[be with you / in a minute]** ______________________________

3 What will your life and world be like in 50 years' time?

► Will-future, p. 224

What do you suppose your life will be like in 50 years' time?
Make meaningful sentences using "probably, suppose, expect, think, I'm afraid, I'm sure".

Example: sit / in front of a monitor / all day
I (do not) think that I / we / people will sit in front of a monitor all day.

1. be / commercials on TV / most of the time ______
2. people / not talk / to each other any more ______
3. use / mobile phones ______
4. go / by car ______
5. live / on Mars ______
6. life / be / more comfortable than today ______

4 What are they going to do next? – Media at work

► Future with 'going to', p. 223

a) **Match the first step in the box below with a suitable second step.**

	▼	First step
1.	c	**The assistant has just written an e-mail.**
2.		The trainee has just opened his / her laptop.
3.		The manager has just looked up a telephone number.
4.		The secretary is just opening the word processing program.
5.		The employee has just bought a sandwich at the cafeteria.
6.		The technical assistant has installed a new program.
7.		The secretary has just written a letter.

	Second step
a)	write a letter
b)	make a call
c)	**send it**
d)	turn it on
e)	test it
f)	put it in an envelope
g)	eat it

b) **Write down what the people in 4 a) are going to do in complete sentences. Use a separate sheet of paper.**

Example: 1. c) The assistant is going to send it.

5 Which media should we use? – A discussion at an advertising agency

► Future with 'going to', p. 223 ► Will-future, p. 224

Fill in the suitable form of 'going to' or 'will' in order to complete the following conversation.

Henry: According to our plans we are going to start the new advertising campaign in time for the winter season. I think it will be best to advertise in local newspapers.

Annie: It is a quality product so I expect that sales [1.] ____________ be better if we advertise in quality magazines.

George: How about radio commercials? Perhaps we [2.] ____________ reach more customers in this way.

Trisha: Don't forget the Internet. It's a product for young people, too. It [3.] ____________ probably be the best way to address them.

Henry: That's a good idea! I [4.] ____________ phone *InterAD* right after our meeting and arrange that.

Annie: Don't forget that George has an appointment with the team from *RadioTeen*. He [5.] ____________ to talk to them about new conditions. Perhaps a mix of radio and Internet advertising [6.] ____________ be best.

6 Managing situations – Talking about the future

M

► Future with 'going to', p. 223 ► Will-future, p. 224

Sie chatten mit einem/r englischsprachigen Freund/in und schreiben, dass ...

1. Sie wahrscheinlich Ihre Prüfung bestehen werden. ____________
2. Sie annehmen, dass es genügend Zeit zum Lernen geben wird. ____________
3. Sie ihn / sie bestimmt in Ihren nächsten Ferien besuchen werden. ____________
4. Sie sich ein neues Computerprogramm gekauft haben und es heute Abend ausprobieren werden. ____________
5. Ihre Mutter Sie gerade gebeten hat, ihr zu helfen, und Sie in zehn Minuten wieder zurück sein werden. ____________

C | Reading: You can't escape it!

7 You can't escape it! → page 52 ► Mit Texten ohne Wörterbuch umgehen, S. 257

Match words from list A with suitable words from list B – according to the texts.

	▼	A
1.		to place
2.		to download
3.		to post
4.		to target
5.		to offer
6.		to pay
7.		to send
8.		to warn
9.		to approach
10.		to use
11.		to commit
12.		to do

	B
a)	ideas
b)	children
c)	students
d)	false identities
e)	Internet users
f)	bets
g)	music
h)	deposits
i)	investigations
j)	rooms
k)	e-mails
l)	a crime

D | Practice

8 What's on the radio? → page 54 ► Vokabeln systematisch lernen, S. 261

Complete the phrases in the list below with one of the words in the box.

of – of – on – out – out – to – to – to – to – with

1.	according	
2.	to check	
3.	in order	
4.	to be aware	
5.	the use	

6.	to find	
7.	to have access	
8.	to be obsessed	
9.	to be addicted	
10.	to have an effect	

9 Training skills – How to describe a cartoon

→ page 55 ► Karikaturen beschreiben und analysieren, S. 244

a) Describe and analyse the following cartoon by filling in suitable words from the box below.

caption – **cartoon** – cartoonist – care – dangers – exaggerates – girl's – Internet – painting – past – publish – puzzled – sitting – social – users – waiting

"Don't worry, daddy already knows and likes you. He's hacked all your social media accounts."

The cartoon shows a living room in which we can see a table, a lamp and a [1.] ______ on the wall. Two young people – a girl and a boy – are [2.] ______ side by side on a sofa behind the coffee table. It looks as if it is the living room of the [3.] ______ parents. The girl is talking to the boy who looks a little [4.] ______. The boy seems to be at his girlfriend's home for the first time and he is [5.] ______ to see the girl's father or the girl's parents. According to the [6.] ______ the girl says: "Don't worry, daddy already knows and likes you. He's hacked all your social media accounts." The [7.] ______ is making fun of the situation. In the [8.] ______ parents did not know a lot about their daughter's or son's friends before they met them but today – regarding all the [9.] ______ networking accounts especially young people have – they can find out a lot more on the [10.] ______ beforehand. Of course, the cartoonist [11.] ______ but there is some truth in the cartoon because young people often [12.] ______ private data and pictures on the Internet which can be seen by other [13.] ______.
I personally know some friends who do not [14.] ______ about their private data and so this cartoon can be a funny way to make them aware of the possible [15.] ______.

P **b) Describe and analyse the following cartoon in a similar way. The words in the box may help you. Use a separate sheet of paper.**

caption – Wi-Fi (wireless Internet)

The cartoon shows ...
The cartoonist is making fun of ...
In my opinion ...

"I've never eaten here. I come for the broadband."

E | Reading +

10 Young people and social media – Crossword

→ page 57

Complete the crossword below with words from the text.

ACROSS

2. the short, thick finger on the side of your hand
4. a person who does s.th. by free choice, usually for little or no payment
6. to relax after a stressful period of time
8. a possibility or choice
9. to stay alive and live on after a dangerous situation
11. impossible to get in contact with
14. a piece of information that is sent to s.o.
15. a computer program that has a special function (short form)
16. to become aware of s.th.

DOWN

1. a cell phone that has additional software functions
3. s.th. you normally do every day
5. placed at the beginning
7. s.o. who creates computer programs
10. the flat part of the inside of your hand
12. a medium level
13. a short period of time when an activity or a job stops

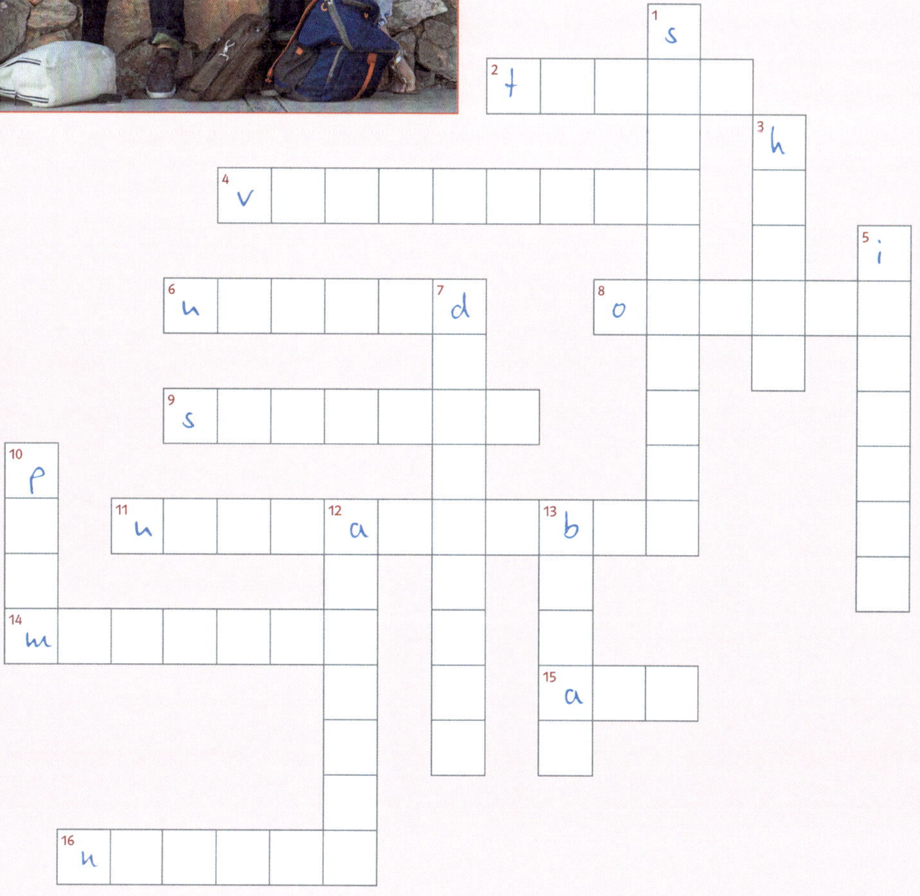

Unit 5

Economic and social changes

A | Getting started: Challenges of a changing society

1 Challenges of a changing society → pages 60 / 61 ► Vokabeln systematisch lernen, S. 261

Find the nouns for the following verbs.

1. to challenge ____
2. to head ____
3. to equal ____
4. to isolate ____
5. to employ ____
6. to apply ____
7. to reject ____
8. to communicate ____
9. to support ____
10. to govern ____
11. to migrate ____
12. to work ____

B | Grammar

2 Living in England ► Defining relative clauses, p. 218

Connect the sentence halves and add "who" or "which" to make defining relative clauses.

1. England is a country …	who which	a) sell cosmetics as well as medicine.
2. Beefeaters are guards …		b) work at the Tower of London.
3. Drugstores are shops …		c) has had some number-one hits.
4. Adele is a singer …		d) lies in the north of England.
5. Leeds is a big city …		**e) has a large number of immigrants.**

1. e) England is a country which has a large number of immigrants.
2. ____
3. ____
4. ____
5. ____

3 Changes at home

► Defining relative clauses, p. 218 ► Non-defining relative clauses, p. 219

Fill in "who" or "which" or leave out the relative pronoun.

According to a report [1.] __________ was published by *Kehily's Insurance* last week, the British are keeping more and more useless things in their homes. Many British homes are half full of stuff [2.] __________ people do not need or want any more. In the last fifty years, rising incomes and technical developments have led to an increasing number of consumer goods [3.] __________ have found their way into our homes but they have not found their way out again. People especially keep electrical devices, clothes and toys because they think that one day they might be able to use them again. Dora Keegan, [4.] __________ is 43, is one of those people [5.] __________ knows that there are far too many things just lying around unused. Why can she not get rid of the things [6.] __________ she does not need any more? "I've checked my house and found that there are computers, radios, bicycles, old clothes and children's toys. But how can I throw away things [7.] __________ cost hundreds of pounds? Nearly all the things [8.] __________ I found are still useable. There's the old doll [9.] __________ belonged to my daughter, the bicycle [10.] __________ can be used by my grandchildren one day or the baby shoes [11.] __________ my mother kept for me. It seems very difficult to leave the past behind."

4 Rules at the National Women's History Museum

► Modal auxiliaries, p. 218

Complete the rules at the Women's History Museum.
Use "must" or "mustn't".

1. **You [take] your bag into the museum.**
2. **You [leave] your bag in a locker.**
3. You **[turn]** your mobile phone off.
4. You **[use]** your mobile phone in the museum.
5. You **[be]** quiet.
6. You **[shout or run]** in the museum.
7. You **[take]** photos in the museum.
8. You **[keep]** a safe distance between you and the pictures.
9. You **[touch]** the pictures.
10. You **[smoke]** inside the building.

1. You mustn't take your bag into the museum.
2. You must leave your bag in a locker.
3. __________
4. __________
5. __________
6. __________
7. __________
8. __________
9. __________
10. __________

5 Everything changes! What will life be like in 100 years' time?

► Modal auxiliaries, p. 218

Note down what you think the world will be like in 100 years' time. Use one of the expressions in the box.

(not) have to – (not) be allowed to –
(not) be able to

Today ...

1. **pupils must go to school.**
2. people can go skiing in the Alps.
3. Americans need not have an identity card.
4. a lot of older people cannot handle a computer.
5. guests must not smoke in restaurants.
6. people may drive cars with a petrol engine.
7. young people may drive a car at the age of 17.

Example:

1. In 100 years' time I think pupils will have to go to school, too. /
Or: In 100 years' time I think pupils will not have to go to school any more.
2. ______
3. ______
4. ______
5. ______
6. ______
7. ______

6 Managing situations – Giving explanations and definitions

► Defining relative clauses, p. 218

Ein englischsprachiger Bekannter versteht einige deutsche Begriffe nicht. Erläutern Sie diese Begriffe unter der Verwendung von Relativsätzen.

1. Berufsschule
2. Fachhochschulreife
3. Klausur
4. Klassenbuch
5. Klassensprecher/in

1. Berufsschule is a college which ...
2. ______
3. ______
4. ______
5. ______

C | Reading – A career waiting for you?

7 Training skills – How to anticipate, skim and scan

► Antizipieren, Skimming, Scanning, S. 256

a) Anticipating:

1. Look at the photo and write down what you think the text may deal with.
   After looking at the photo I think the text may deal with ...
2. Look at the heading of the text and write down your ideas about the text.
   After reading the heading I think the text is about ...

b) Skimming: Read the text below quickly to find out if your ideas in a) 1. und a) 2. were right. Tick the suitable box and give a reason for your answer.

☐ My ideas about the text were right (because) ...
☐ My ideas about the text were not right (because) ...

R **c) Scanning: Read the text again and find out about the facts in 1.–8.**

HOW IT ALL DEVELOPED

Originally the Greek name for school meant "leisure". Today schools are institutions which pupils in most countries must attend. Formal schools have a long history: they existed in Greece and China more than 2,000 years ago. Islam was another culture which developed a school system. At first, children prayed and learned at mosques, but in the ninth century separate schools were introduced. In Europe during the Middle Ages schools mainly taught Latin. This led to the expression "grammar school", which still exists in Britain. But many children did not attend school because they had to work. It was only in 1880 that education for 5-to-10-year-old children became compulsory in Britain. In 1944 the school-leaving age was raised to 15 and schools were divided into primary and secondary schools. This is still the case today so pupils leave primary school at the age of 11. Many of the earlier schools in Europe and North America were one-room schools where one teacher taught pupils of all ages in the same classroom. From the 1920s on schools became larger institutions with several classrooms, offices, gyms and – in the past few decades – even computer labs.

1. The original meaning of the word "school" .... leisure
2. The age of the school system .... _____
3. The original place for children to learn in Islam .... _____
4. The subject pupils learned in the Middle Ages .... _____
5. "Grammar school" is a term that is still used in .... _____
6. The year in which all children had to go to school for the first time in Britain .. _____
7. The age at which pupils start going to secondary school in Britain .... _____
8. The number of classrooms in earlier schools .... _____

M **d) Sie bereiten eine Präsentation zum Thema „Schulen früher und heute" für Ihren Geschichtsunterricht vor. Entnehmen Sie die entsprechenden Informationen aus dem obenstehenden Artikel. Formulieren Sie ganze deutsche Sätze.** ► Mediation, S. 254

8 A career waiting for you? ► Vokabeln systematisch lernen, S. 261

Make phrases – as they are used on pages 64 and 65 – by completing the verbs in the list below with words in the box.

about – about – about – at – for – from – out – out – out – through – up – up – with – with – with – with

1. to go ________
2. to be ________
3. to skim ________
4. to look ________
5. to point ________
6. to pick ________
7. to catch ________
8. to speak ________
9. to stress ________
10. to worry ________
11. to go ________
12. to cope ________
13. to suffer ________
14. to think ________
15. to match ________
16. to apply ________

9 From college to work – not an easy road → page 65

Fill in suitable phrases from task 8 to write a short summary of the text. Watch out for the correct tenses and forms.

The text "From college to work – not an easy road"

[1.] ________ the problems of young people today. Lots of them are [2.] ________ their uncertain future and are [3.] ________ bad job perspectives. Increasing academic pressure often [4.] ________ them ________. Because of their financial problems many students have to do part-time jobs which makes it more difficult to [5.] ________ the academic work at college. As they do not want to lose social contact they often [6.] ________ with friends in the evening although there is little free time. One way to take time out from this stress is to [7.] ________ a voluntary activity in a foreign country – a so-called gap year.

D | Practice

10 Problems of the modern welfare state → page 66 ► Vokabeln systematisch lernen, S. 261

Some words often go together. Match the following words from list A with words from list B to make phrases as they are used in the listening text.

A

1. professor of ________
2. welfare ________
3. medical ________
4. pension ________
5. old-age ________
6. social ________
7. senior ________
8. family ________
9. National ________
10. unemployment ________
11. public ________
12. people in ________

B

a) treatment
b) pension
c) structure
d) economics
e) citizen
f) benefits
g) insurance
h) state
i) need
j) scheme
k) Health Service
l) services

11 Technological and economic development

Use suitable words to say what the pictures below represent.

1. ______________________

2. ______________________

3. ______________________

4. ______________________

5. ______________________

6. ______________________

E | Reading +

12 Industry 4.0 – Crossword → page 68 / 69

Complete the crossword below and find the solution by filling in the corresponding English words from the text for their German equivalents.

1. erhöhen, vergrößern
2. Motorhaube
3. ersetzen
4. umwandeln
5. Abstimmung, Koordinierung
6. Zunahme
7. Produktivität
8. Fortschritt
9. untersuchen
10. menschlich
11. führen, lenken
12. Wirkung, Einfluss
13. (sich) anpassen
14. (sich) ausbreiten

Solution ▼

1.																	
2.																	
3.																	
4.																	
5.																	
6.																	
7.																	
8.																	
9.																	
10.																	
11.																	
12.																	
13.																	
14.																	

Unit B

Starting a placement in London

1 Showing the way

a) **You are standing at a bus stop close to Hungerford Bridge and ask a man for help. He tells you the way to Westminster Abbey. Choose six of the sentences below and put them in the right order to find the way.**

	A	Turn left into Horse Guards.		F	On your right you find the Houses of Parliament.
	B	Go down Victoria Embankment.		G	Turn right into Bridge Street.
	C	Turn left at the traffic lights.		H	Then you can see Westminster Abbey on your right.
	D	Go past Big Ben.		I	Go past Parliament Square.
	E	Take the Queen's Walk along the Thames.		J	Cross Westminster Bridge.

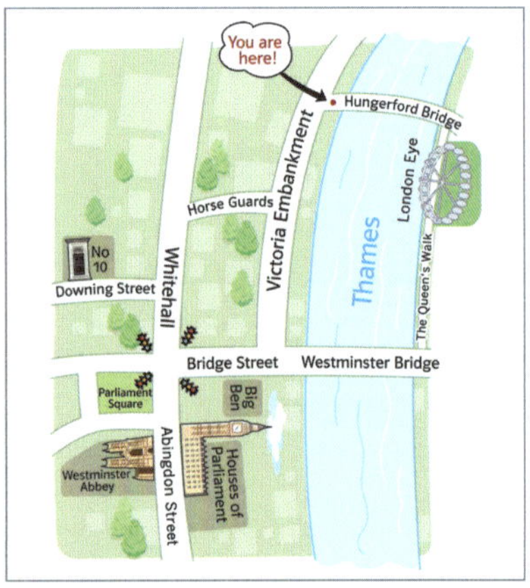

b) **After visiting Westminster Abbey you are in Abingdon Street now and ask a passer-by the way to the London Eye. Complete the following sentences so that it is easy to find the way.**

1. First go down ______
2. At the traffic lights ______
3. Then go down ______
4. Go past ______
5. Cross ______
6. After crossing ______
7. Soon ______

2 A new guest

Complete the following dialogue between a landlady of a guesthouse and a guest by filling in suitable words from the box.

call – else – easily – fine – from – I'm – may – meet – on – pleasant – pleased – serve – tired – welcome

Guest: Hello, I'm Frederik Smaland [1.] ______ Sweden.

Landlady: [2.] ______ to Southend Guesthouse, Frederik. [3.] ______ Samantha Fox.

Guest: [4.] ______ to meet you, Ms Fox.

Landlady: Nice to [5.] ______ you, too. Please [6.] ______ me Samantha. Did you have a [7.] ______ journey?

Guest: I had no problems at all. The train arrived [8.] ______ time and I found your guesthouse [9.] ______.

Landlady: That's [10.] ______________. [11.] ______________ I show you your room now?

Guest: That would be nice. What time do you [12.] ______________ breakfast?

Landlady: From eight to nine. Is there anything [13.] ______________ I can do for you?

Guest: Thanks very much. I'm a bit [14.] ______________. I think I'll go to bed now. Good night.

3 Introducing people

Fill in the gaps in the following bubbles with words from the box.

come – from – introduce – meet –
myself – name – pleased – this

1. Nice to ______________ you.

2. Let me ______________ you to Mr Conrad.

3. Ms Davids, ______________ is Susan Doyle.

4. ______________ to meet you.

5. Let me introduce ______________.

6. My ______________ is Mel.

7. Where are you ______________?

8. I ______________ from Bristol.

4 Showing people around

Look at the plan of the company on page 75 of your student's book and complete the following description with suitable words from the box.

in front – next – behind – between – the left – far – the back

1. The front office is right ______________ the entrance.
2. The front office is ______________ of the general office.
3. The general office is ______________ the toilets and the personnel manager's office.
4. The cafeteria is ______________ to the kitchen.
5. The general manager's office is not ______________ away from the executive suite.
6. You'll find the stores at ______________ of the building.
7. You can see the logistics manager's office on ______________ there.

Unit 6

Ecology and economy

A | Getting started: We are all part of it!

1 Tackling climate change → page 76 ► Vokabeln systematisch lernen, S. 261

Some words often go together. Match the following words from list A with words from list B to make terms as they are used in the text.

A	▼			▼	
1.		greenhouse	7.		solar
2.		fossil	8.		carbon
3.		food	9.		weather
4.		global	10.		summer
5.		sun's	11.		CO_2
6.		degrees	12.		climate

B			
a)	emissions	g)	supply
b)	energy	h)	levels
c)	conditions	i)	Centigrade
d)	effect	j)	change
e)	footprint	k)	panel
f)	fuels	l)	temperatures

B | Grammar

2 Reporting what people said ► Reported speech, p. 225

Match the statements in reported speech with the corresponding statements in direct speech.

	▼	Direct speech: Last week …
1.	b	**Jonathan said: "I came here yesterday."**
2.		Lily and Emily said: "We don't know where he is."
3.		Oliver and Sue said: "We came here yesterday."
4.		Mohammed said to Cindy: "I like my new mobile phone."
5.		Gerald said to Lucy: "I like your new mobile phone."
6.		Sophie said: "I don't know where he is."
7.		Jill said: "I'm coming tomorrow."
8.		Olivia said: "I needn't do it."
9.		Daniel and Katie said: "We will discuss this topic tomorrow."

	Reported speech: He / she / they said (that) …
a)	she did not have to do it.
b)	**he had come there the day before.**
c)	she did not know where he was.
d)	she was coming the following day.
e)	they had come there the day before.
f)	he liked her new mobile phone.
g)	they would discuss that topic the following day.
h)	he liked his new mobile phone.
i)	they did not know where he was.

3 After a nature presentation ► Reported speech, p. 225

Derek took part in a nature presentation last week and now wants to tell his friends what the presenter said. Use the phrases below and write what Derek tells his friends.

This is part of the presentation:

"**[1.]** Welcome to my nature presentation! **[2.]** Thank you all for coming. **[3.]** Some days ago I was right here and I found this place ideal for the meeting today. **[4.]** I want to show you the beauty and the problems of our environment. **[5.]** This tree next to me is a good example. **[6.]** It has grown for many years. **[7.]** It is protecting us from the sunshine during the presentation. **[8.]** But it doesn't look as good as it did some years ago. **[9.]** Air pollution has made it difficult for many species to survive. **[10.]** Perhaps within only a few generations there will be no trees here any more. **[11.]** It is my aim to stop this development. **[12.]** I know that you are all here to help!"

(The presenter ...) – said that – went on to say that – told us that – informed us that – stated that – added that – concluded that ...

1. The presenter welcomed us to his nature presentation.
2. He thanked us all for coming.
3. The presenter said that some days before he had been right there and had ...
4. He went on to say that ...
5.
6.
7.
8.
9.
10.
11.
12.

4 *GreenLife*'s FAQ-page

► Reported speech, p. 225

Report what the following visitors to *GreenLife*'s home page wanted to know.

1 EmmaFX: **Has *GreenLife* already tried to help the panda?**

2 Drago21: **Where can I join the group?**

3 Drizzlezizzle: Did you take part in the latest demonstration for tuna?

4 Foxy1a: Is there a local group?

5 TreeTop: When did *GreenLife* become international?

6 EnviroTwo: Do you work together with other organizations?

7 LogoLogo: Where will the meeting take place next week?

8 DesmondDes: How much money do you get from companies?

9 Wishywashy: Are you also dealing with the water problems in the Third World?

1. EmmaFX wanted to know if GreenLife had already tried to help the panda.
2. Drago21 asked where he could / was able to join the group.
3. ______
4. ______
5. ______
6. ______
7. ______
8. ______
9. ______

5 Managing situations – Reporting a TV documentary

► Reported speech, p. 225

Sie haben im Fernsehen einen interessanten Film über die zukünftige Entwicklung unserer Erde gesehen. Die Wissenschaftler in dem Beitrag haben u. a. das Folgende gesagt:

1. „Wir haben neue Ergebnisse gefunden."
2. „Wir hoffen, dass wir in der Lage sein werden, der Umwelt zu helfen."
3. „Wir arbeiten gerade hart an den Problemen."
4. „Unsere Lösungen werden eine Menge Geld kosten."
5. „Wir haben vor einer Woche mit dem Präsidenten über unsere Pläne gesprochen."

Berichten Sie einem/r englischsprachigen Bekannten über das, was die Wissenschaftler gesagt haben.

1. The scientists stated that ...
2. ______
3. ______
4. ______
5. ______

C | Reading: Where does our food come from?

6 You are what you eat → page 80 ► Vokabeln systematisch lernen, S. 261

Find the missing verbs or nouns for the following words in the text.

	Verb	Noun
1.		production
2.	to live	
3.	to consume	
4.	to develop	
5.	to compete	
6.		standard
7.		expectations
8.	to taste	

	Verb	Noun
9.	to react	
10.	to offer	
11.		contribution
12.	to pollute	
13.		modification
14.		label
15.	to protect	
16.	to challenge	

7 Training skills – How to work with a dictionary

► Mit dem Wörterbuch arbeiten, S. 258

a) **Put the words in the box into alphabetical order.**

economist – ecosystem – ecstatic – **ecological** – ecology – economic – economics – ecstasy – economy – ecologist – economical – economize

1. ecological
2. ______
3. ______
4. ______
5. ______
6. ______
7. ______
8. ______
9. ______
10. ______
11. ______
12. ______

b) **Look up the words in exercise a) in a dictionary and put them into the appropriate box below.**

Nouns	Adjectives	Verbs
economist		

c) **Look up the pronunciation of the words above and decide where to put the main stress (first, second or third syllable). Mark the syllable that is stressed.**

d) Look up the words in exercise a) in an English-English dictionary and match them with the following definitions.

1. ecological ______ concerning the relationships between plants, animals, people and their environment; causing minimal damage to the environment
2. ______ a person who studies the relationships between plants, animals, people and their environment; a person who specializes in ecology
3. ______ extreme feeling of great happiness; an illegal drug in pill form
4. ______ concerning the organization of the money, industry and trade of a country
5. ______ a person who studies, teaches or writes about economics
6. ______ the study of the production and consumption of goods and services in a society
7. ______ the organizational system or the management of the money, industry and trade of a country
8. ______ to save money by spending it carefully; to make economical use of sth., to avoid waste
9. ______ saving money or time or effort; not wasteful
10. ______ all of the plants and animals in a particular area and the complex relations between them and their environment; an ecological community together with its environment
11. ______ showing or feeling great happiness
12. ______ the study of relationships between plants, animals, people and their environment; the study of living things, their environment and the relations between them

e) Look up the words in exercise a) in a German-English dictionary and match the words with their German meanings.

1. Begeisterung, Ekstase ecstasy ______
2. Ökologie, Umweltschutz, Umweltforschung ______
3. sparsam, wirtschaftlich ______
4. Wirtschaft, Ökonomie ______
5. Wirtschaftswissenschaften, Wirtschaftslehre ______
6. verzückt, ekstatisch ______
7. Ökologe, Ökologin, Umweltschützer/in ______
8. Ökosystem, Naturhaushalt ______
9. sparen, haushalten, sparsam wirtschaften ______
10. ökologisch, Umwelt- ______
11. ökonomisch, wirtschaftlich ______
12. Wirtschaftswissenschaftler/in, Volkswirt/in, Ökonom/in ______

D | Practice

8 Consuming the world → page 82 ► Vokabeln systematisch lernen, S. 261

A2.10

a) Put the following words from the listening task under a suitable heading.

climate change – violence – supermarket – soil erosion – railway – trade – instability – flight – goods – lack of fresh water – road – products – overfishing – demand – conflict

Economy	Transportation	Ecological effects	Political effects

b) Complete the list above with words that you remember from past tasks.

E | Reading +: Saving nature

9 Earth has lost half its wildlife → page 85 ► Mit Texten ohne Wörterbuch umgehen, S. 257

Find suitable verbs in the text and put them in the correct box.

	Definition / Explanation	Verb
1.	divide into two equal parts	
2.	make unclean, contaminate	
3.	damage so badly that it cannot be repaired	
4.	supply, make available	
5.	defend, save, keep from being harmed	
6.	make, manufacture	
7.	get a general idea of the size, use mathematical processes	
8.	study closely and carefully	

	Definition / Explanation	Verb
9.	consume completely	
10.	move water from or to a particular place	
11.	send out, give off	
12.	take in s.th. in a natural way	
13.	drop sharply	
14.	get rid of, leave rubbish	
15.	bring a product into a country	
16.	make certain, make sure	

Unit 7

Energy, technology and employment

A | Getting started: Cleaner energy

1 Scotland – fossil-free by 2030? → page 89 ► Vokabeln systematisch lernen, S. 261

Complete the following list with words which you can find in the text.

Fossil fuels	Renewable sources of energy	Energy sources available in and around Scotland

B | Grammar

2 Technology at home ► Passive voice, p. 227

What can or cannot be done? What must or must not be done? What should or should not be done? Make meaningful or funny sentences. Use the words from the table below. Use a separate sheet of paper.

1. Bread	keep	cooker
2. Milk	toast	laptop
3. Soup	write	dishwasher
4. Plates	make	toaster
5. E-mails	cook	telephone
6. Calls	clean	refrigerator

Example of a meaningful sentence:

Bread can be toasted in the toaster.

Example of a funny sentence:

Calls should not be made in the dishwasher.

3 How an easy chicken noodle soup is made

► Passive voice, p. 227

Write the steps below in the passive voice.

What you need for an easy chicken soup:
1 chicken, 3 large potatoes, 2 carrots,
200 g small noodles, 1 teaspoon salt,
2 pieces of chicken bouillon, 2 spoons dried or fresh parsley (*Petersilie*)

What must be done:
1. **First clean the chicken under running water.**
2. Then boil the chicken in 6 cups of salt water until the chicken is fully cooked.
3. Take the chicken out and cut it into pieces.
4. Peel the potatoes and cut them into small pieces.
5. Prepare the carrots in the same way.
6. Add chicken bouillon and cook the potatoes, carrots and chicken for twenty minutes.
7. At the end add the noodles and cook them until they are tender.
8. Decorate the soup with parsley.

1. First the chicken is cleaned under running water.
2. Then the chicken ...
3.
4.
5.
6.
7.
8.

4 Chocolate

► Passive voice, p. 227

Rewrite the report about chocolate. Use the passive voice for the underlined verbs. Fill in the by-agent where necessary. Use a separate sheet of paper.

In 1828 Van Houten [1.] **invented** the method of producing cocoa powder. He [2.] mixed this powder with sugar and [3.] made a drink that tasted delicious. Some years later an English company [4.] produced and sold the first chocolate bar. In 1875 a Swiss manufacturer [5.] made the first milk chocolate.

Today most people [6.] love chocolate. Last year chocolate lovers in the UK [7.] spent over 5 billion pounds. US consumers [8.] ate about half of the world's chocolate production. The Swiss eat the most chocolate per person – they [9.] consume more than 10 kg per person per year.

1. In 1828 the method of producing cocoa powder was invented by ...
2. This powder ...

5 Developments

► Passive voice, p. 227

a) Match the following pictures with the inventions on the right.

1

2

3

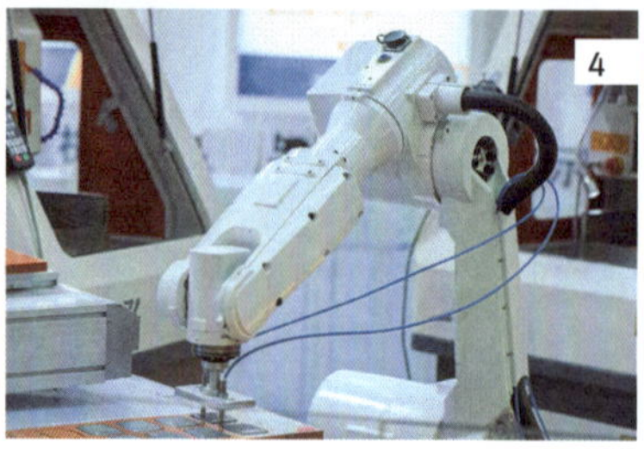
4

5

☐ stone tools
☐ robot
☐ wheel
☐ metal tools
☐ printing press

b) Complete the following text by filling in a suitable form of the passive voice.

In the beginning stone tools **[1. use]** *were used*. That is why this era **[2. call]** ____________ the "Stone Age". At about that time, the use of fire **[3. discover]** ____________. After metal tools **[4. invent]** ____________ about 10,000 years ago many things became easier. The production of energy and transportation **[5. revolutionize]** ____________ when the wheel **[6. invent]** ____________ about 6,000 years ago. A big step forward **[7. make]** ____________ when the printing press **[8. develop]** ____________. In the last few hundred years our lives **[9. change]** ____________ by many other important inventions. Today our work **[10. do]** ____________ by robots and our children **[11. entertain]** ____________ by TV or video games. Let us hope for the future that everyone's life **[12. make]** ____________ more comfortable and safer by new inventions which **[13. cannot / even / think]** ____________ of today.

6 Managing situations – Explaining regulations and notes

M

► Passive voice, p. 227

Sie werden von einem englischsprechenden Ausländer angesprochen, der wissen möchte, was die folgenden Inschriften auf Schildern bedeuten. Erläutern Sie diese unter der Verwendung des Passivs.

Example:

1. *Credit cards are not accepted.*
2. ____________
3. ____________
4. ____________

C | Reading: Energy sources of the future

7 Different views

→ page 92 ► Mit Texten ohne Wörterbuch umgehen, S. 257

Match the following nouns from the texts on page 92 of your student's book with suitable definitions.

	▼	Noun from the text
1.		unemployment
2.		statement
3.		opportunity
4.		fuel
5.		tide
6.		resource
7.		turbine
8.		plant
9.		breakwater
10.		project
11.		emphasis
12.		impact

	Definition
a)	a good chance
b)	wall that is built out into the sea to protect a harbour or beach
c)	natural source of supply
d)	building or factory where s.th. is made
e)	engine with blades that are moved by wind or water
f)	the state of not having a job
g)	regular upward and downward movement of the level of the sea
h)	planned piece of work that has a specific purpose
i)	a powerful and often negative effect
j)	s.th. you say or write in a formal way – opinion that you express
k)	material that is burned to produce heat or power
l)	special importance or attention given to s.th.

D | Practice

8 Office technology

► Mit Texten ohne Wörterbuch umgehen, S. 257

Complete the following text about office technology by filling in suitable words from the box below.

box – carbon paper – communication – copies – e-mails – Internet – inventions – landline – mobile – technology – telephone – typewriter

Office technology has come a long way. The use of modern [1.] ______ has made office work much easier today. In the old days, people had to write everything by hand and then the [2.] ______ came along which was much quicker. However, if people needed [3.] ______ of a letter they were typing, they had to use [4.] ______. Office work changed a lot when the [5.] ______ was more widely used and [6.] ______ became even faster. Of course, this device was not the [7.] ______ phone as we know it today; it was still only the [8.] '______ telephone' and when people were travelling and wanted to call someone, they had to find a phone [9.] ______. Nowadays business letters have largely been replaced by [10.] ______. People can work anywhere in the world – all they need is [11.] ______ access. However, communication [12.] ______ still continues to change. So what will the next step be?

9 Training skills – How to write a composition

a) "Modern technology does not really make life better." Underline the arguments below in two different colours. Use green for arguments for and red for arguments against modern technology.

- creates new jobs
- replaces workers with computers and robots
- makes work more efficient
- makes hard work easier with the help of machinery
- lets machines do the dirty and dangerous work
- increases unemployment
- increases international competitiveness
- connects people worldwide through information technology and new or faster forms of transport
- has led to weapons of mass destruction
- access to information is easier
- uses a lot of energy
- communication has become cheaper, quicker and more efficient
- developing countries cannot afford advanced technology
- people in developing countries are still dying of hunger
- people must learn new skills for the new production methods
- makes life easier
- medical science saves lives
- it is becoming more and more complex and difficult to handle

b) Choose those three arguments for and against modern technology that you think are the most important.

P **c) Copy the following table into your exercise book and write your composition.**

Heading **Modern technology does not really make life better**
Introduction We are all surrounded by modern technology today. We work on computers, communicate by Internet or mobile phone and can watch football matches on TV that are taking place right now thousands of miles away. This …
Arguments against / for the statement Some people argue that … On the other hand …
Your point of view I think … In conclusion I would like to …

1. Complete the introduction.
2. Use the arguments that you have chosen in b) and write them down in complete sentences. First write down arguments which do not correspond to your opinion. Then state the arguments which express your opinion. Use connectives from the first *Help* box in your student's book on page 93.
3. In conclusion, state your opinion. Use phrases from the second *Help* box on page 93.
4. Check what you have written.

E | Reading +: Shops without shop assistants

10 The automated future – Crossword → page 97

Complete the crossword below by filling in words from the text on page 97 of your student's book.

ACROSS

1. Beschäftige/r, Mitarbeiter/in
5. Steuern
6. Verlust
8. Einzelhandel
10. Kunde, Kundin
12. wohlhabend, florierend
13. männlich
15. Ungleichheit
16. steuern, lenken
19. Filiale
20. ungelernt
21. Palette
22. Arbeit

DOWN

2. beseitigen, eliminieren
3. Lager(halle)
4. Lohn, Gehalt
7. (Lager) auffüllen
9. Wettbewerb, Konkurrenz
11. Anstieg
14. Aufsichtsperson, Abteilungsleiter/in
17. Transportwagen, Einkaufswagen
18. vertrauen

Unit 8
The service industry

A | Getting started

1 Careers in tourism and leisure
→ page 101 ► Mit Texten ohne Wörterbuch umgehen, S. 257

Fill in the gaps of the following summary with suitable words from the text.

While other people are going on holidays in the summer people working in the [1.] ____________ and [2.] ____________ industry experience a busy time. Many new jobs have been created in this business area so there are many [3.] ____________ to find work today. Working in the tourism industry can give you the chance to [4.] ____________ to far-away countries but there is also a wide [5.] ____________ of jobs in England. When you apply for a job it could be helpful to have a university [6.] ____________ or if you already have some job [7.] ____________ in the tourism industry but most of all new employees must have excellent [8.] ____________ [9.] ____________. They must always be aware that tourists come [10.] ____________.
Pawan Durani thinks that a job in the tourism industry is very [11.] ____________ and can be much [12.] ____________. He has already visited the Far [13.] ____________ and Central America and has got to know a lot of typical tourist [14.] ____________ all over the world. He believes that the practical training is just as important as the [15.] ____________ he has learnt on several courses.

B | Grammar

2 Too late? ► Conditionals, p. 226

The Barker family are going on a trip to Majorca tomorrow. Write down in complete sentences what will happen to them if they do or do not do certain things. Use the phrases in the order given and watch out for the tenses.

1. alarm clock does not ring
2. the Barkers get up late
3. they are in a hurry
4. they forget their passports
5. they are not able to check in at the airport
6. the Barkers decide to drive home to get their passports
7. they are not in time for their flight
8. they spend their holidays in England
9. they do not have as much sunshine
10. the children do not get sunburned
11. they do not suffer from skin problems when they are older

1. If the alarm clock does not ring, the Barkers will get up late.
2. If the Barkers get up late, they will be ...
3.
4.
5.
6.
7.
8.
9.
10.

So it will be better for the Barker family if the alarm clock does not ring in the morning.

3 What would happen if ... ? ► Conditionals, p. 226

Make if-sentences as in the example.

1. **rain / not play badminton**
   If it rained, I would not play badminton.
2. have money / buy a car
3. be sick / not go on holidays
4. (Toby) like football / watch it on TV
5. (Mandy) go on holiday to the USA / visit the White House
6. (Roberta and Sue) live in London / go shopping a lot
7. (Dave and Allen) go to Ireland / travel by ferry
8. (Vance) have a driving licence / go by motorbike

4 Transport in the past and in the future

► Conditionals, p. 226

a) Match suitable parts of the following sentences.

1.	c	**If Columbus's ship had sunk,**	**a)**	if – you – not start – now
2.		If someone invents a very fast spaceship,	**b)**	driving – be – less dangerous
3.		The oil reserves would last longer	**c)**	**he – not discover – America**
4.		If people drove more slowly,	**d)**	if – Gottlieb Daimler – not have – the idea
5.		Fewer people would travel by plane	**e)**	if – cars – consume – less petrol
6.		Someone else would have invented the car	**f)**	if – flights – be – more expensive
7.		Columbus would not have been able to search for India	**g)**	we – be able – travel – to other galaxies
8.		There would be more road accidents	**h)**	if – the Queen – not give – him the money
9		You will never reach your aim	**i)**	if – people – buy – more cars

b) Write the above parts in complete sentences. Watch out for the different tenses.

1. If Columbus's ship had sunk, he wouldn't have discovered America.
2.
3.
4.
5.
6.
7.
8.
9.

5 Managing situations – Going to the USA ► Conditionals, p. 226

Sie wollen eine Reise in die USA machen und übermitteln in einem Internet-Chat einem amerikanischen Freund einige Informationen, die Ihnen eine Mitarbeiterin im Reisebüro gegeben hat. Benutzen Sie dabei „*if*"-Sätze.

1. **„Sie werden im Internet einchecken können, wenn Sie Zeit sparen wollen."**
2. „Wenn Sie im Hotel frühstücken wollen, werden Sie zusätzlich $10 bezahlen müssen."
3. „Wenn Sie mit einem Partner verreisten, würde die Reise billiger für Sie sein."
4. „Wenn Sie vor einer Woche gekommen wären, hätte ich ein besonderes Angebot gehabt."
5. „Sie werden $300 mehr bezahlen müssen, wenn Sie direkt nach Washington fliegen wollen."

1. I will be able to check in via Internet if I want to save time.
2. If I want ...
3.
4.
5.

C | Reading: Mass tourism

6 Training skills – How to answer questions on a text

a) **Find out which tenses are used in the following questions.**

	Question	Tenses	Answer
1.	**Where did the Waltons travel last year?**	past simple	**Hawaii**
2.	Where do many Germans usually spend their holidays?		Germany
3.	When did the President visit India?		two months ago
4.	Where will you go at Christmas?		Austria
5.	What countries have been popular in the past few years?		Spain, France
6.	Where had the Prime Minister been before he went to Canada? (2 tenses)		Alaska
7.	Where was his wife staying at that time?		New York
8.	Why are the holiday makers leaving?		because of the rain

b) **Answer the questions above in complete sentences. Be careful about the tenses. Use a separate sheet of paper.**

1. The Waltons travelled to Hawaii last year.

7 It's not only sunshine and fun – Crossword → page 104

Fill in the crossword puzzle with suitable English words which you find in the text.

ACROSS

6. behandeln
7. Reserven
8. Verbraucher/in
10. Einnahmen
12. beitragen
13. Risiko
16. Umwelt
17. Erwärmung
19. Emission, Ausstoß
20. Grundwasser
22. Saison
23. unterstützen
24. Entfernung

DOWN

1. benötigen
2. Urlaubsort
3. Wirkung, Effekt
4. Reiseziel
5. Attraktion
9. verschmutzen, vergiften
11. Brunnen
14. Knappheit
15. gewaltig, enorm
18. (Umwelt-) Verschmutzung
21. Regen

D | Practice

8 Fitness and work

► Vokabeln systematisch lernen, S. 261

a) **Fill in the nouns that correspond to the adjectives and verbs in the table.**

b) **Find out the common endings for each groups of nouns.**

	Adjective	Noun
1.	fit	
2.	well	
3.	busy	
4.	happy	
	Common ending	

	Adjective	Noun
5.	obese	
6.	responsible	
7.	popular	
8.	active	
	Common ending	

	Verb	Noun
9.	to agree	
10.	to manage	
11.	to employ	
12.	to equip	
	Common ending	

	Verb	Noun
13.	to recommend	
14.	to inform	
15.	to confirm	
16.	to qualify	
	Common ending	

E | Reading +: Serving people

9 Living on $2.13 an hour and tips

→ page 108 / 109 ► Mit Texten ohne Wörterbuch umgehen, S. 257

Find synonyms for the following words or expressions in the text. Note down the line in which you have found the synonym.

1. the money that you get for working – ______________ (line ___)
2. things that you can eat – ______________ (line ___)
3. every day – ______________ (line ___)
4. people who buy things – ______________ (line ___)
5. money that you have to pay for living in a flat – ______________ (line ___)
6. remember – ______________ (line ___)
7. per hour – ______________ (line ___)
8. in reality – ______________ (line ___)
9. curriculum vitae (CV) – ______________ (line ___)
10. rise – ______________ (line ___)

Unit 9

Living and working in a globalized world

A | Getting started: Migrant workers

1 What's your story? → page 113 ► Mit Texten ohne Wörterbuch umgehen, S. 257

Match the following words from the comments with their explanations by connecting them with lines.

	Word from the text
1.	benefits
2.	expatriate (expat)
3.	national insurance contributions
4.	prejudice
5.	nationality
6.	accent
7.	skin
8.	tax
9.	immigrate

	Explanation
a)	status of being a member of a particular nation
b)	money which you pay to the state to receive a pension at old age and other benefits
c)	a feeling of dislike for a person or group of people because of their race, sex or religion
d)	come to a country to live there
e)	the natural outer covering of the body of a person or animal
f)	a charge on persons or property which has to be paid to the government for public purposes
g)	money that is paid by the government when someone becomes sick or stops working
h)	person (mostly British or American) who leaves their country to live/work in another one (often for a certain time period)
i)	way of pronouncing words which is typical for people in a particular region or country

B | Grammar

2 A meeting of a One World group ► Infinitive, p. 227

Desmond Truly took part in an information evening held by a local One World group last night. At home he tells his parents what the speaker, Mrs Wilson, said. Report Desmond's statements and use one of the verbs from the box below.

want – make – expect – ask – advise – tell – let

1. "Inform as many people as possible about our group."
2. "Don't leave the poor countries alone with their problems."
3. "Think about the ways you can help."
4. "Please come to our next meeting."

5. "Let's watch the new film about Central Africa."
6. "Don't look the other way when there are people in need."
7. "Please have a cup of tea in the break."
8. "Help with our future activities, please."

1. Mrs Wilson wanted us to inform as many people as possible about their group.
2. She asked us not to ...
3. She made us ...
4. ______
5. ______
6. ______
7. ______
8. ______

3 What do you prefer? ► Gerund, p. 228

At the weekend Desmond went to the One World shop because he wanted to offer his help. He met Debbie, who had already been working there for some years.

In their conversation about their hobbies and interests Desmond mentioned the following things. Write about Desmond. Use the words in brackets.

1. **"It's nice to watch films on TV." [like]**
   Desmond likes watching films on TV.
2. "I don't really think that basketball is interesting to watch." **[dislike]**
   ______
3. "I like my skates but I like my bike even better." **[prefer]**
   ______
4. "I can't stand those people who have nothing to do. I don't want to just hang around." **[hate]**
   ______
5. "It's nice to talk to you, Debbie." **[enjoy]**
   ______
6. "I really want to help other people and I enjoy that very much." **[love]**
   ______

4 Helping at the One World shop ► Gerund, p. 228

a) **Complete the following phrases with a suitable preposition from the box.**

at – for – of – of – of – of – in – in – to

1. **be afraid** of	4. look forward ______	7. be tired ______
2. have the chance ______	5. succeed ______	8. apologize ______
3. be good ______	6. have the opportunity ______	9. have difficulty ______

b) **This is what Debbie said when she met Desmond at the shop. Rewrite her statements. Use the phrases in exercise a).**

1. **We can change the world a little.**
   We have the chance/opportunity of changing the world a little.
2. Sometimes it is not easy for us to find new members. ______
3. I don't want to make too many mistakes. ______
4. We managed to raise £800 at the last meeting. ______
5. I think in July we'll have a nice barbecue. ______
6. I am sorry if I talk too much. ______

C | Reading: Profits or ethics?

5 Working conditions ► Mit Texten ohne Wörterbuch umgehen, S. 257

Fill in the following summary about working conditions in the textile industry with one of the adjectives or adverbs in the box.

cheap(ly) – inadequate(ly) – invisible(-bly) – large(ly) – legal(ly) – poor(ly) – proper(ly) – real(ly)

Thousands of sewing machines can be heard again in workshops around Britain but the workers cannot be seen: they are [1.] ______ to the public because they work in backyards. About 12,000 workers, mostly women, are employed in this sector and are not [2.] ______ paid – they only receive three pounds an hour or even less. The working conditions are [3.] ______ bad, they are [4.] ______ for a developed country. Of course, paying less than the minimum wage is not [5.] ______ but many women from Asia or Eastern Europe only speak English [6.] ______. So this is their only chance to contribute to their household income. Companies want to save money so they are interested in producing as [7.] ______ as possible. And their workers pay the price, a problem that is [8.] ______ common not only in Britain, but also in other European countries and beyond.

6 £3 per hour! A fair deal? → page 116

Complete the following lists with words from the text.

1. **People:** a) empl______ b) fas______ des______ c) res______ d) wom______ e) chil______
2. **Organizations and businesses:** a) tex______ ind______ b) comp______ c) gar______ ind______ d) ret______

3. **Conditions:** a) hea_______ and saf_______ sta_______ b) bul_______ c) toi_______ bre_______
d) empl_______ cont_______ e) work_______ rig_______
4. **Money:** a) wa_______ b) mat_______ pa_______ c) lab_______ co_______ d) inc_______
5. **Buildings and machinery:** a) fac_______ b) sh_______ c) works_______ d) sew_______ mac_______

7 Training skills – How to do mediation exercises ► Mediation, S. 254

Sie haben die Aufgabe, für Ihren Unterricht einen Vortrag über Bangladesch auf Deutsch vorzubereiten. Sie haben in einer Internet-Enzyklopädie den folgenden Text gefunden.

a) **Ordnen Sie dem Text über Bangladesch diese Überschriften zu.**

Regierungssystem – Wirtschaft – Bevölkerung – Geografie – Geschichte

Bangladesh

A _______________

Bangladesh is a country in South Asia. It is surrounded by India in the west, north and east and by Myanmar in the east. Bangladesh opens to the Bay of Bengal in the south, which leads into the Indian Ocean. The country covers an area of 56,977 square miles, which is less than half the size of Germany. Most parts are less than 12 m above sea level – most of the land is flat and very fertile. Bangladesh is also called the land of rivers.

B _______________

For hundreds of years the area called Bengal belonged to the British Empire. From the beginning of the 20th century on there was a call for independent states there. After World War II the western part of Bengal became part of India and the eastern part had to join Pakistan. After a civil war Bangladesh declared its independence in 1971.

C _______________

Today, Bangladesh, which is officially called the People's Republic of Bangladesh, is a parliamentary democratic state. Its capital is Dhaka. After some unrest following independence Sheik Hasina became Prime Minister and head of government for the third time in 2014 in a largely fair election.

D _______________

In the last 50 years the population of Bangladesh has doubled. Now the country has more than 150 million inhabitants, which makes it 8th in the world by population. As the country is relatively small this means that Bangladesh is one of the most densely populated countries. The official language is Bengali while English is used as a second language. The vast majority (about 85 %) of Bangladeshi are Muslims.

E _______________

Bangladesh is a developing country. Its currency is the Taka. Bangladesh is still an important agricultural producer with emphasis on rice, tea, jute and fruit. The industrial sector includes the textile industry which makes up 70 % of the country's export earnings. But all in all Bangladesh is a poor country. With only a few thousand dollars income per person it is about the 150th "richest" nation in the world. About 25 % of the population still live below the international poverty line, which means that people live on less than US$ 1.25 per day.

b) **Markieren Sie in den jeweiligen Abschnitten die wichtigsten Informationen.**

M c) **Sammeln Sie in Ihrem Heft diese Stichpunkte auf Deutsch unter den fünf vorgegebenen Überschriften als Grundlage für Ihren Vortrag über Bangladesch.**

D | Practice

8 Globalization ► Vokabeln systematisch lernen, S. 261

Find suitable verbs or nouns for the following words.

	Verb	Noun
1.	to grow	
2.		production
3.	to export	
4.		sale
5.	to demand	
6.		attention
7.	to state	
8.		commitment
9.	to protect	
10.		existence
11.	to shop	
12.		improvement

	Verb	Noun
13.	to dress	
14.		label
15.	to change	
16.		trainers
17.	to enable	
18.		globalization
19.	to organize	
20.		cooperation
21.	to communicate	
22.		movement
23.	to manage	
24.		costs

E | Reading +: We are the change!

9 Not all Asian clothing factories are unethical – Crossword → page 120 / 121

Complete the crossword on the opposite page by filling in English words from the text.

ACROSS

2. örtlich, lokal
5. Armut
7. nützlich
9. Missbrauch
11. Nachhaltigkeit
15. Fußabdruck
17. Rohstoff, Bodenschatz
18. Bekleidung

DOWN

1. Fabrik, Mühle
3. Baumwolle
4. Ausbeutung
5. Herstellung, Produktion
6. Anforderungen
8. Kunde
10. Mode
12. Wohltätigkeit (sorganisation)
13. Kollege, Kollegin
14. Unglück
16. benötigen, fordern
19. behandeln

10 Managing situations – Writing a blog in English

► Infinitive, p. 227 ► Gerund, p. 228

Sie schreiben einen internationalen Blog auf Englisch, in dem Sie auch andere Menschen überzeugen wollen, dass sie etwas für eine gerechtere Welt tun können. Schreiben Sie auf Englisch, dass …

1. **es Ihnen gefällt, im 21. Jahrhundert zu leben.**
2. Sie nun die Chance haben, viele Menschen zu informieren.
3. Sie nicht wollen, dass die Menschen in der Dritten Welt an Hunger leiden.
4. Sie darum bitten, Fairtrade-Produkte zu kaufen.
5. Sie sich darauf freuen, vielen Kindern damit zu helfen.
6. der Gedanke daran Sie auf eine bessere Welt hoffen lässt.

1. I enjoy living in the 21st century.
2. ______
3. ______
4. ______
5. ______
6. ______

Unit 10

International organizations and politics

A | Getting started: Our needs and our rights

1 Are we all born equal and free? → page 125 ► Vokabeln systematisch lernen, S. 261

Fill in suitable words from list B to make meaningful expressions in list A. You can find these expressions in the text.

	A		B
1.	human	a)	rights
2.	international	b)	states
3.	Declaration of	c)	agreements
4.	United	d)	speech
5.	member	e)	the law
6.	political	f)	organizations
7.	freedom of	g)	rights
8.	equality before	h)	education
9.	right to	i)	Nations
10.	social	j)	participation
11.	non-governmental	k)	International
12.	Amnesty	l)	security

B | Grammar

2 Life in Nicaragua ► Participle, p. 228

Read the following report by Rita, a young woman working in Nicaragua. Replace the underlined phrases in the report. Use the present or past participle.

I have lived in the country [1.] which is officially called the Republic of Nicaragua for three years now. It is the largest country in Central America. The region [2.] which lies close to the Caribbean Sea is my favourite part of the country. One quarter of the population [3.] that lives in Nicaragua lives in Managua – the capital of Nicaragua. Most of the population, [4.] which totals nearly six million, speaks Spanish. In 1502 Columbus was the first European to reach this region. In the 16th century the Spanish founded some important towns here but most of the Indian civilization, [5.] which was destroyed by the Spanish, has disappeared. Today Nicaragua is independent. Many people here are rather poor. There is a high unemployment rate and those [6.] who have jobs only earn little money. Food is cheap, but products [7.] which are made in the USA cost even more than there. A pair of jeans costs 30% more than in the US! Nevertheless, the cost of living for me is very low and there is a lot I like about Nicaragua. Tourists and people [8.] who live here can enjoy fresh food and great beaches. Politics, on the other hand, is always a problem here.

1. I have lived in the country officially called the Republic of Nicaragua for three years.
2. The region lying close to the Caribbean Sea is my favourite part of the country.
3. One quarter of the population ______
4. Most of the population ______
5. Most of the Indian civilization ______
6. There is a high unemployment rate and those ______
7. Food is cheap, but products ______
8. Tourists and people ______

3 Getting to know Nicaragua

► Participle, p. 228

A lot of things happened to Rita after moving to Nicaragua. Join the pairs of sentences and use the present participle.

1. Rita heard a lot about Nicaragua. Then she decided to live there.
   After hearing a lot about Nicaragua Rita decided to live there.
2. She wanted to know as much as possible about Nicaragua. So she did a lot of research into the country.
   Wanting to know ...
3. She went to Nicaragua. Before that she sold her car.
   Before ______
4. She looked for a place to live for a few days. Then she rented a small house.
   After ______
5. Rita worked for a US company first. She met a lot of US Americans.
   While ______
6. She is very open-minded. So she soon found friends in Nicaragua.
   ______
7. She wanted to get to know the country better. So Rita bought an old motorbike.
   ______
8. She has had so many nice experiences in Nicaragua. So Rita wants to stay there forever.
   After ______

4 Humanitarian help for the Third World

► Infinitive, p. 227 ► Gerund, p. 228 ► Participle, p. 228

Complete the following text. Fill in the infinitive with or without "to", the gerund or a participle of the verbs in brackets.

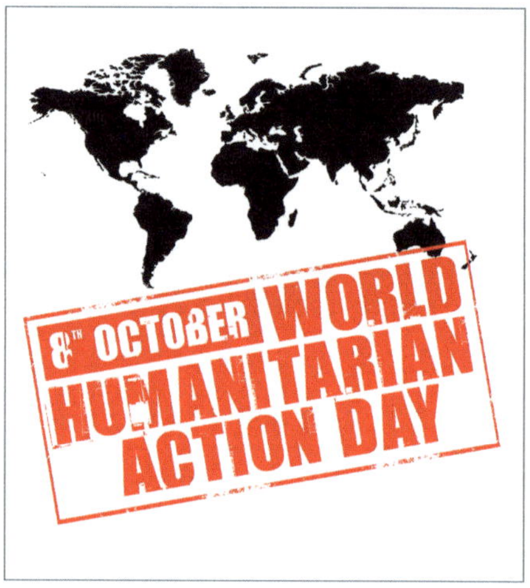

Your help is needed!

After **[1. lose]** losing their homes, about 300,000 Tamils are at present living in the worst possible conditions. One of the reasons **[2. cause]** __________ these conditions at the moment is the conflict with the government in Sri Lanka. However, heavy rain and floods have also made the Tamils **[3. leave]** __________ their homes. Many people suffer from malaria and other illnesses are increasing, too. The refugees are very poor and need urgent help. After **[4. be attacked]** __________ by different militant groups, most international aid groups have left the conflict area for safety reasons. As the government is not interested in **[5. help]** __________ the refugees there are only some local groups left **[6. try]** __________ to help, but they need our assistance.
That is why we want to make people **[7. join]** __________ our action day on 8 October.
We are asking you **[8. come]** __________ to our information evening on the night before.
You have the opportunity of **[9. offer]** __________ help in the way you can do best. Maybe you are good at **[10. collect]** __________ money or you want to assist us at our information desk. Perhaps you are good at **[11. create]** __________ home pages? We must all be interested in **[12. provide]** __________ a minimum standard of living for everyone. We still enjoy **[13. live]** __________ in peace but this can change when there is trouble around us.
Let us **[14. help]** __________ other people and in a way we can also do something for ourselves and for our children at the same time.

5 Managing situations – Creating a homepage for your One-World-Group

M

► Infinitive, p. 227 ► Gerund, p. 228 ► Participle, p. 228

Sie gestalten die Homepage Ihrer Eine-Welt-Gruppe in Deutsch und in Englisch.
Übertragen Sie in Ihrem Heft den folgenden deutschen Text ins Englische.

Hallo!
Hast du keine Lust mehr, deine Abende vor dem Fernseher zu verbringen?
Hast du Interesse daran, mit jungen Leuten zusammenzuarbeiten?
Hilfst du gerne anderen Leuten, denen es finanziell weniger gut geht als dir oder die gesundheitliche Probleme haben?

Wenn die Antworten auf diese Fragen „ja" sind, dann werde Mitglied in unserer Eine-Welt-Gruppe. Bei regelmäßigen Treffen wirst Du allen möglichen jungen Leuten begegnen. Außerdem hast Du die Möglichkeit, Mitglieder von Gruppen aus anderen Ländern kennenzulernen.

C | Reading: Human rights and mass surveillance

6 Mass surveillance threatens human rights

→ page 128 ► Vokabeln systematisch lernen, S. 261

Find corresponding verbs, adjectives or nouns for the following words from the text.

	Verb	Adjective	Noun
1.	to create		
2.			security
3.		wide	
4.	to collect		
5.			information
6.		effective	
7.	to realize		
8.			suspicion
9.		weak	
10.	to save		
11.			use
12.		worried	
13.	to protect		
14.			stability
15.		global	
16.			practice

7 Training skills – How to write a summary

► Eine Inhaltsangabe schreiben, S. 235

R **a) Read the text carefully and match the paragraphs (A – F) with the following headings.**

1. *Facebook*'s reasons for publishing the reports
2. *Facebook* report: Increasing number of governmental data enquiries
3. Benefits of the Internet in the past
4. *NSA* affairs show that governments have used private data
5. Negative features of the Internet today
6. *Facebook* report: Growing number of content restrictions

Facebook says governments' requests for user data are on the rise

by Thomas Wilson, *The Political Newspaper*, 13 November 2016

(A) Only years ago the Internet was seen as a powerful tool to strengthen the values of democracy. The Internet was not only seen as a tool to improve the spread of information for citizens but also to promote political participation.

(B) But ever since the *NSA* scandals, revealed by whistle-blower Edward Snowden in 2013, government access to private data has started a discussion about the violation of privacy all around the world. So in the following years the communication technology industry with some of its leading companies like *Facebook*, *Microsoft*, *Yahoo* and *Alphabet Inc* has insisted on greater transparency on governments requesting data.

(C) In the Global Government Requests Report posted on its website the social networking service *Facebook* has revealed that government requests for user account data increased by 18 % in the first half of 2015 to 41,214 account requests up from 35,051 requests in the previous year. The report contains information about 93 countries in the period from January to June this year. Most of the account requests – more than 60 % – came from agencies in the United States. However, European countries, like the United Kingdom, Germany, Italy and France, also made up extremely high numbers of data requests in 2015.

(D) In its report *Facebook* also uncovered that it had to remove more than twice the amount of posts and other content from its website than in the year before. The majority of requests for content-related takedowns came from countries like India and Turkey, because they were either violating local laws or showed violent crimes. But also Germany has asked *Facebook* to restrict some posts, because they violated Germany's prohibition of Nazi propaganda. A comparison with last year's report shows that content limitations have increased by 112 %.

(E) With its 1.5 billion users, *Facebook* has started to publish half-yearly reports listing the number of times governments have asked the company for information on its users. Chris Sonderby, Deputy General Counsel at *Facebook*, said they were releasing the report because they wanted to provide more transparency for their users. Governments have more and more relied on *Facebook's* outstanding amount of user data to help prevent and investigate crimes. Moreover, *Facebook* pointed out they do not provide governments with so-called "back-doors", giving access to computer programs bypassing their security mechanisms.

(F) All in all, the Global Government Requests Report shows that today the Internet is not only seen as a promotor for democratic systems but it also seems to be a threat to some of its cornerstones: freedom of privacy, freedom of speech and freedom of information.

(440 words)

b) Match some of the expressions Thomas Wilson uses in the text with alternative expressions. Fill in the corresponding letter of the alternative.

	Original	▼		Alternative
1.	The Internet was seen as a powerful tool to strengthen the values of democracy.		a)	Firms demand that governmental requests for data should be shown publicly.
2.	Companies have insisted on greater transparency on governments requesting data.		b)	Crime prevention has led governments to count on *Facebook*'s plenty of user data.
3.	Most of the account requests – more than 60 % – came from agencies in the United States.		c)	The amount of content-related removals has more than doubled.
4.	They had to remove more than twice the amount of posts and other content.		d)	The World Wide Web was regarded as an influential instrument to support the principles of democracy.
5.	Governments have more and more relied on *Facebook*'s outstanding amount of user data to help prevent and investigate crimes.		e)	The Web puts some of democracy's pillars at risk.
6.	The Internet seems to be a threat to some of democracy's cornerstones.		f)	At least three out of five requests were made by the United States.

c) Read the summary below. Then fill in the gaps with suitable words from the text.

The newspaper comment "*Facebook* says governments' requests for user data are on the rise" written by **[1.]** ______________ and published in **[2.]** ______________ on **[3.]** ______________ is about the latest *Facebook* report on the growing number of requests for **[4.]** ______________ by governments all over the world.

First the author points out the benefits of the **[5.]** ______________ in the past. It clearly wanted to promote the basic principles of **[6.]** ______________. However, in the meantime the **[7.]** ______________ affairs show us how governments have used private data. This is why the **[8.]** ______________ calls for more **[9.]** ______________ with governmental data requests. The author moves on to discuss the findings of the **[10.]** ______________ report. He shows that there has been an increasing number of data requests from **[11.]** ______________, and especially by **[12.]** ______________. The *Facebook* report also reveals that the number of **[13.]** ______________ has doubled. The author goes on to outline *Facebook*'s reasons for publishing the reports. On the one hand, *Facebook* wants to create transparency for its users and to show that *Facebook* does not **[14.]** ______________ governments with "back-doors". On the other hand, *Facebook* also wants to show that governments now increasingly count on *Facebook*'s user data in crime prevention. Finally, the author mentions some of the dangers of the Internet today. In his opinion it can put important **[15.]** ______________ of our democracy at risk such as our **[16.]** ______________ of privacy, speech and information.

D | Practice

8 Political participation in the UK

► Vokabeln systematisch lernen, S. 261

Put the corresponding nouns in the boxes. Nouns which are in the same group use a common ending. Find these common endings and write them in the spaces under the boxes.

1.	discuss	
2.	decide	
3.	restrict	
4.	express	
5.	constitute	
6.	move	
7.	introduce	
8.	divide	
Common ending		

13.	examine	
14.	participate	
15.	publicize	
16.	present	
17.	discriminate	
18.	specify	
19.	motivate	
20.	declare	
Common ending		

9.	judge	
10.	develop	
11.	assign	
12.	argue	
Common ending		

21.	authorize	
22.	equalize	
23.	humanize	
24.	nationalize	
Common ending		

E | Reading +: The EU and refugees

9 Migrant boat disaster – Antonyms

→ page 132 / 133 ► Vokabeln systematisch lernen, S. 261

Find antonyms in the text for the words in the box below.

1.	closed	
2.	danger	
3.	births	
4.	emigration	
5.	harmless	
6.	confident	
7.	outside	
8.	sent	
9.	push	
10.	illegal	
11.	long-term	
12.	bright	

13.	hinder	
14.	unsystematic	
15.	private	
16.	unsafe	
17.	unlocked	
18.	exit	

10 Migrant boat disaster – Crossword → page 132 / 133

Complete the crossword below and find the solution by filling in the corresponding English words from the text.

1. Schutz
2. Programm, Maßnahme, Plan
3. Schmuggler
4. militärisch
5. ankündigen
6. Strom, Gezeitenstrom
7. Maßnahme
8. Vorgehen
9. Rettung
10. verletzlich, verwundbar
11. Verurteilung, Verdammung
12. Flüchtling
13. Notfall, Notsituation
14. Friedhof

Solution ▼

1.																	
2.																	
3.																	
4.																	
5.																	
6.																	
7.																	
8.																	
9.																	
10.																	
11.																	
12.																	
13.																	
14.																	

Unit C

Doing a placement in London

1 Making arrangements on the phone

Put the following parts of the telephone calls into the correct order.

1.

	A	I'd like to speak to Susan Atkins.
	B	Peter Jones speaking.
	C	*Nonfood UK*. How can I help you?
	D	Thanks.
	E	Who's calling, please?
	F	Just a moment, Mr Jones. I'll put you through.

2.

	A	Thanks, I'm fine.
	B	Hello Susan. This is Richard.
	C	What can I do for you, Richard?
	D	Susan Atkins.
	E	Hello Richard. Nice to hear from you again. How are you?
	F	Well, I wonder if it is possible to arrange a meeting for next week.

3.

	A	Well, I'm out on Tuesday morning. Could you manage Tuesday afternoon?
	B	What about next Tuesday?
	C	That suits me, too. I look forward to seeing you then.
	D	Just a moment. Let me get my diary – you said Tuesday?
	E	Right. Would Tuesday morning be OK?
	F	Yes, Tuesday afternoon would suit me fine. Shall we say three o'clock?

2 Helping people

Some business people visiting *Nonfood UK* need help or advice. Match their requests with suitable answers.

		Guest's request
	A	Could you make a copy for me?
	B	I need a taxi.
	C	Do you have Wi-Fi here?
	D	I'd like to speak to Mr Morgan.
	E	I need to wash my hands.

	Your answer
F	No problem. Just take the second door on the right.
G	It's a free service for our guests. The code is DX-5439gH.
H	Yes, of course. I'll call Jason to do that for you.
I	Just a moment. I'll call one for you.
J	I'll inform him that you've arrived.

3 Writing business letters and personal letters

The following parts of a business letter and a personal letter are mixed up.
Note "B" for business letter and "P" for personal letter in front of the phrases.
Then write the two letters in the right order into your exercise book.

	A	Best wishes		I	If you have any further questions, do not hesitate to contact us.
	B	How are you?		J	Yours sincerely
	C	Just let me know if it suits you.		K	Tina
	D	We are pleased to send you our catalogue and price list.		L	Thank you for your enquiry dated 3 November.
	E	Hi Mark		M	Dear Mr Peters
	F	We look forward to receiving your order soon.		N	Susan Doyle
	G	Sales assistant		O	Give me a call on 03452345234.
	H	I'm writing because I've lost your phone number.		P	I'm coming over to your place next summer and it would be great to see you again.

4 Writing a business e-mail

Complete the following e-mail by filling in suitable words from the box. Then put the sentences in the right order and copy the text into your exercise book.

arrive – assistant – call – could – dear – delighted – receiving – sincerely – thank

1. ______________ you arrange to see Mr Winterbottom in your office at 2 p.m.?
2. Donna Nobis
   Sales ______________
3. ______________ you very much for yesterday's call.
4. ______________ Ms Middleton
5. Yours ______________
6. Your telephone ______________ of 20 September 20…
7. Looking forward to ______________ your answer by next Friday.
8. He will ______________ at Glasgow International Airport at 11 a.m.
9. Mr Winterbottom will be ______________ to meet you in Glasgow on 10 October.

Unit 11

Enquiries

1 Finding synonyms → page 142

Match the words on the left with words on the right which have a similar meaning. For help refer to the substitution table on page 142 of your student's book.

b)	1.	understand
	2.	receive
	3.	manufacture
	4.	first-class
	5.	particularly
	6.	conditions
	7.	state
	8.	offer
	9.	expectations
	10.	soon
	11.	answer

a)	high-quality
b)	learn
c)	reply
d)	obtain
e)	produce
f)	especially
g)	requirements
h)	in the near future
i)	quotation
j)	quote
k)	terms

2 Completing a letter

Fill in suitable words to complete the following enquiry.

[1.] ____________ Mr Chang

Your [2.] ____________ in the *Export Times*

We [3.] ____________ that you have a wide [4.] ____________ of musical instruments.
Your company has been [5.] ____________ by a friend.
We are a young and rapidly [6.] ____________ importer of such items and are
[7.] ____________ for a reliable [8.] ____________ of standard quality at reasonable
[9.] ____________. Please let us [10.] ____________ your terms of payment and
[11.] ____________. Please also [12.] ____________ your delivery
[13.] ____________ and possible [14.] ____________ on large orders.
If your prices are [15.] ____________, we will be [16.] ____________ to place
substantial [17.] ____________.
We look forward to [18.] ____________ your answer in the [19.] ____________ future.
Yours [20.] ____________

3 Finding the suitable preposition

Fill in suitable prepositions from the box.

about – by – for – in – of – of – of – of – to – to

1. we refer ________ an advertisement
2. a range ________ products
3. it was recommended ________ a customer
4. we are looking ________ a partner
5. we are interested ________ your products
6. we would like to know ________ your terms
7. terms ________ payment
8. a manufacturer ________ first-class products
9. a sample ________ your products
10. looking forward ________ receiving your answer

4 Telephoning – An enquiry on the phone

Match the following questions on the telephone with suitable answers.

		Questions		Answers
	1.	How can I help you?	a)	Shipment will be executed FOB Calcutta.
	2.	Which instruments are you especially interested in?	b)	We are looking for a reliable supplier of musical instruments.
	3.	Which models would you recommend?	c)	We can grant a quantity discount of 10% on orders over €10,000.
	4.	Could you please state your terms of delivery?	d)	It's P – E – T – E Y – O – R – K.
	5.	Do you offer any discounts?	e)	The goods could be delivered by the end of August at the latest.
	6.	Can you spell your name, please?	f)	We would like to know more about your range of bongos.
	7.	What is your earliest date of delivery?	g)	I think the models "Haiti" and "Hawaii" will meet your requirements best.

5 Mediation – Enquiries

M

Schreiben Sie in einer Anfrage an einen Möbelhersteller in Schweden, dass Sie …

1. sich auf die Website der Firma beziehen.

____

2. ein bedeutender Möbelimporteur mit Sitz in der Nähe von Kiel sind.

____

3. sich insbesondere für traditionelle skandinavische *(Scandinavian)* Möbel interessieren.

____

4. gerne die Qualität der Produkte testen würden.

____

5. einen Besuch Ihres Einkaufsleiters in der Fabrik des Herstellers in Schweden arrangieren möchten.

____

6. größere Aufträge in Aussicht stellen können, wenn die Waren Ihren Erwartungen entsprechen.

____

Unit 12

Offers

1 Completing an offer → page 149

Complete the following offer. Fill in suitable words from the e-mail on page 149 of your student's book.

Dear Mr Tucker

We refer to your [1.] ______________ of March 10.

We can make the following [2.] ______________. Our [3.] ______________ quoted are FOB Hamburg. We can grant you a [4.] ______________ of 10% on all orders over €10,000. Payment must be executed by letter of [5.] ______________. Attached you can find our [6.] ______________ and our price [7.] ______________. Please [8.] ______________ us if you have any questions. Your order will be executed [9.] ______________.

We look [10.] ______________ to receiving your order soon.

Yours [11.] ______________

2 Offers – Crossword

Fill in the corresponding English words.

ACROSS

3. Kunde
4. frei an Bord *(abbreviation)*
6. Menge
8. begrüßen, willkommen heißen
10. bar, Sofortzahlung
11. handeln mit
14. Anforderungen
17. unterbreiten
19. versichern
20. Preisliste
21. netto, ohne Abzug

DOWN

1. gewähren
2. in Verbindung treten
3. Kosten, Versicherung, Fracht *(abbreviation)*
5. gültig
6. Angebot
7. Katalog
9. fest
12. Rabatt
13. zögern
15. ab Werk *(abbreviation)*
16. durchführen, ausführen
18. verzollt geliefert *(abbreviation)*

3 Telephoning – An offer on the phone

Put the following parts of a telephone call in a suitable order.
Fill in numbers from 1 to 12.

	A	Yes, of course. Everything was fine with your latest delivery.
	B	Hello, Heather. This is Christopher. How are you?
	C	That's perfect, Heather. Thanks for your help.
	D	*Davids & Sons*. Heather Mirren speaking. How can I help you?
	E	It's a pleasure, Christopher. Have a nice day.
	F	Yes, they really sell well. Do you need model X1 or X2?
	G	Well, as our stocks are running low we want to place a further order for your DigiCam X.
	H	Well, 200 of your X1 version and 100 of the X2 type.
	I	X1 – 200 pieces, X2 – 100 pieces. No problem. You should have the cameras by the end of the month.
	J	Thanks, I'm fine, Christopher. Did our shipment arrive on time last week?
	K	Bye, Heather.
	L	I'm glad to hear that. What can I do for you today, Christopher?

4 Mediation – Offers

M

Schreiben Sie in einem Angebot an einen Interessenten in den USA, dass Sie ...

1. sich für die Anfrage des Unternehmens bedanken.
2. zurzeit ein Sonderangebot unterbreiten können.
3. die Zahlung innerhalb von vier Wochen nach Lieferung erwarten.
4. mit LKW sofort liefern können.
5. für Aufträge bis zum Ende des Monats 10 % Rabatt einräumen können.
6. bereit sind, kostenlose Muster zu senden, damit die amerikanische Firma die Qualität prüfen kann.
7. ein großes Sortiment von weiteren Produkten anbieten können.
8. wie gewünscht den neuesten Katalog senden.
9. Aufträge prompt und sorgfältig ausführen.

Unit 13

Orders

1 Matching words → page 158

Complete the following expressions by filling in suitable nouns from the box on the right. For help refer to the substitution table on page 158 of your student's book.

business – delivery – discount – goods – offer – order – payment – quotation – receipt

1. thank for an ______________
2. place an ______________
3. supply ______________
4. execute ______________
5. effect ______________
6. note from a ______________
7. grant a ______________
8. acknowledge ______________
9. do ______________

2 Completing an order → page 158

Complete the following extract from an order with the correct form of suitable verbs from the substitution table on page 158 of your student's book.

Thank your for your offer of September 23.
We are pleased to [1.] ______________ the attached order. Please [2.] ______________ the following products on the terms stated below. Delivery must be [3.] ______________ by October 20. Payment will be [4.] ______________ on delivery. Please [5.] ______________ this order by return and [6.] ______________ us when the goods have been [7.] ______________.
We [8.] ______________ forward to [9.] ______________ business with you.

3 Dealing with terms of payment

a) **Match the following terms of payment with the suitable explanations.**

		Terms of payment: Payment can be made …
	1.	in advance.
	2.	cash against documents.
	3.	by transfer of the invoice amount within 30 days after receipt of goods.
	4.	on delivery / on receipt of goods.
	5.	with order.
	6.	by irrevocable, confirmed letter of credit.

	Explanation:
a)	Payment is made when the goods arrive.
b)	The buyer pays when he / she orders the goods.
c)	The importer's bank opens an L / C and sends it to the exporter's bank which guarantees payment. The exporter then hands the shipping documents to his / her bank which sends them to the importer's bank. Here the importer can collect the shipping documents against payment.
d)	Payment is carried out when the shipping documents are handed out.
e)	The customer pays before delivery.
f)	The buyer tells his / her bank to transfer money from his / her account to the seller's account.

b) List the terms of payment in exercise a) under the following headings.

Before delivery	On delivery	After delivery

4 Telephoning – Placing an order on the phone

Fill in the gaps in the telephone dialogue with suitable phrases from the box.

you're welcome, Ms Fisher – this will help us a lot – how are you? – hang on a moment, Ms Fisher – we need some of your products urgently – we'll do our best to help you, Ms Fisher – good morning, Mr Tuncay – I wonder if you could send us 5,000 more within the next two weeks – we can send you the items by air within 10 days on our usual terms – how can I help you? – I'm fine

Mr Tuncay: Hello. *Tuncay Export*, Istanbul. **[1.]** ____________

Ms Fisher: Denise Fisher from *Incopex*, Birmingham. **[2.]** ____________

Mr Tuncay: Oh hello, Ms Fisher. **[3.]** ____________

Ms Fisher: Thanks, Mr Tuncay. **[4.]** ____________.
I'm calling because **[5.]** ____________. I hope you can help me.

Mr Tuncay: **[6.]** ____________. Which products can we send you?

Ms Fisher: Well, your summer shirts are selling very well at the moment. **[7.]** ____________

Mr Tuncay: **[8.]** ____________. I'll check our stocks on the computer. ... Ms Fisher? **[9.]** ____________

Ms Fisher: That's great, Mr Tuncay. **[10.]** ____________

Mr Tuncay: **[11.]** ____________. We are always there for you.

5 Mediation – Orders

M

Schreiben Sie in einer Bestellung an ein Unternehmen in Großbritannien, dass ...

1. Sie sich für das Angebot des Unternehmens bedanken.
2. die Preise und Bedingungen Ihren Erwartungen entsprechen.
3. Sie aber einen Einführungsrabatt von 5 % erwarten.
4. die Lieferung FOB Hull erfolgen soll.
5. die Zahlung gegen Übergabe der Frachtpapiere erfolgen wird.

Unit 14

Complaints

1 Complaints – Crossword

Fill in the corresponding English words.

ACROSS

2. Zufriedenheit
4. benötigen
5. auspacken
6. Kiste
9. Beschwerde, Mängelrüge
11. verantwortlich
13. überfällig
14. Reduzierung, Herabsetzung
15. Angelegenheit
18. Inhalt
19. untersuchen
20. vertrauen
21. rückgängig machen, löschen

DOWN

1. defekt
2. beilegen, regeln
3. Behälter
7. Ersatz
8. Verlust
10. bereit
12. Lieferung
14. bedauern
16. fehlend
17. beschädigt
18. Karton

2 Finding the right preposition

Complete the following sentences with the prepositions in the box.

by – for – forward – from – into – on – to – to – with – within

Dear Mr Hilton

I'm writing **[1.]** ____________ you **[2.]** ____________ reference **[3.]** ____________ our order no. RW437.

We ordered the consignment **[4.]** ____________ December 4 and it should have been delivered **[5.]** ____________ January 15. Please look **[6.]** ____________ this matter immediately. Should you not be able to deliver **[7.]** ____________ two weeks, we will have to look **[8.]** ____________ another supplier.

We look **[9.]** ____________ to hearing **[10.]** ____________ you soon.

Yours sincerely

Josh Klingenthal

3 Telephoning – A complaint on the phone

Write the following telephone dialogue in complete sentences.

	Rita Dunkel (Deutschland) ...		Dave Pearson (Canada) ...
1.	meldet sich mit ihrem Namen und fragt, wie sie helfen kann.	2.	meldet sich ebenfalls und bezieht sich auf seinen Auftrag vom 25. Mai.
3.	fragt, ob ihre Lieferung zu seiner Zufriedenheit ausgefallen ist.	4.	antwortet, dass die Lieferung leider Anlass zu einer Mängelrüge gibt.
5.	fragt, was genau passiert ist.	6.	antwortet, dass die falsche Ware geliefert wurde und man die Ware dringend benötigt.
7.	bedauert den Fehler, sichert die sofortige Bearbeitung der Angelegenheit zu und verspricht einen Preisnachlass von 20 %.	8.	bedankt sich und hofft, dass die bestellte Ware innerhalb von zwei Wochen eintrifft.

4 Mediation – Complaints

M

Schreiben Sie in einer Mängelrüge an ein Unternehmen in Südafrika, dass ...

1. deren Lieferung gestern eingetroffen ist.
2. die Ware nicht zu Ihrer Zufriedenheit ausgefallen ist.
3. die Qualität nicht dem Standard entspricht, den Sie erwarten.
4. Sie bereit sind, die Ware zu einem reduzierten Preis zu behalten.
5. Sie hoffen, bald von Ihrem Lieferanten eine Antwort zu erhalten.

Unit 15

Reminders

1 Working with words → page 174

a) **Find the corresponding nouns or verbs for the following words. For help refer to the substitution table on page 174 of your student's book.**

	Verb	Noun
1.	to remind	
2.	to pay	
3.	to attend	
4.	to deliver	
5.	to touch	
6.	to settle	
7.	to refer	
8.	to record	

	Verb	Noun
9.		information
10.		receipt
11.		show
12.		dispatch
13.		hesitation
14.		requirement
15.		enclosure
16.		agreement

b) **Complete the following reminder with words from the table above. Use the right forms of the words.**

Dear Ms Springer

Our records [1.] ______________ that we have not [2.] ______________ payment for our invoice no. 49871/01 yet.

The goods were [3.] ______________ on February 2. According to the terms you [4.] ______________ on [5.] ______________ should have been made by March 2.

I am [6.] ______________ a copy of our invoice for your [7.] ______________. This is probably a simple oversight on your part but please [8.] ______________ your account immediately. Should you [9.] ______________ any further information, do not [10.] ______________ to get in [11.] ______________ with us. We look forward to an early [12.] ______________ of your account.

Yours sincerely

2 Spelling commercial terms

All the words below are written with double letters. Fill in the missing letters as in the example. If you have completed the words correctly, you can read the names of two big cities in Italy and in Portugal.

1. e ff ect
2. usua _ _ y
3. overl _ _ k
4. so _ _ y
5. m _ _ ting
6. co _ _ ection
7. a _ _ ount
8. str _ _ t
9. su _ _ lier
10. g _ _ ds
11. a _ _ ive
12. a _ _ ach
13. s _ _ n

1 F	2	3	4	5	6	7	8

9	10	11	12	13

3 Telephoning – A reminder on the phone

Put the following parts of a telephone call in a suitable order.
Fill in numbers from 1 to 13.

	A	It's my pleasure, Cara. How are you?
	B	Bye, Peter. Have a nice day.
	C	Thanks, Peter. I'm fine. What can I do for you, Peter?
	D	Hello, Peter. Nice to hear from you again.
	E	That's very kind of you, Cara. I knew it was only a simple mistake.
	F	One moment, Peter. I'll just check it on the computer. – Oh, I'm terribly sorry! There seems to be an oversight on our part, Peter. I'll deal with that immediately. You'll receive payment as soon as possible.
	G	Hello. *Irish Superstores Ltd.* Cara Sheridan speaking. How can I help you?
	H	Never mind, Cara. Thank you for your help. I'm looking forward to your payment. Bye, Cara.
	I	Oh yes, I remember, Peter. The consignment was OK. – Anything wrong with it?
	J	I'm phoning about our consignment of deep freezers that we sent you last month.
	K	Hello, Cara. This is Peter Landsberg from *Elektro-Großgeräte* Singen.
	L	Yes, I'm sorry but we haven't received payment yet. I'm sure you've overlooked this.
	M	Of course, Peter. I apologize for the trouble we have caused. I hope it will never happen again.

4 Mediation – Reminders

M

Schreiben Sie in einer Erinnerung an ein Unternehmen in Irland, dass ...

1. Sie darüber informieren möchten, dass bisher keine Zahlung eingegangen ist.

   ____

2. der Auftrag vor zwei Monaten ausgeführt wurde.

   ____

3. Sie eine Kopie der Rechnung als Anlage senden.

   ____

4. Sie weitere Lieferungen einstellen werden, wenn die Zahlung nicht bis zum 7. Mai erfolgt.

   ____

   ____

5. Sie das irische Unternehmen bitten, Kontakt mit Ihnen aufzunehmen, falls es weitere Fragen bezüglich der Zahlung hat.

   ____

   ____

6. Sie sich auf einen schnellen Ausgleich des Kontos des irischen Unternehmens freuen.

   ____

   ____

Unit 16

Perspectives after college

A | Reception

1 Listening comprehension

A 3.15

Listen to the interview with Samantha Young and complete the sentences with information from the interview.

1. Samantha went to the job centre in Sheffield because ______ ______ and because ______.
2. She received an offer for an apprenticeship with ______ ______.
3. The company's headquarters are in Manchester because ______ ______.
4. Samantha moved to Manchester because ______ ______.
5. While doing her apprenticeship she does not only work for the company but she also ______ ______.
6. Samantha advises other young people to ______ ______.

2 Reading comprehension

School-leavers and graduates: how to write your first CV

[…] You've finished years of education and it's time to enter the world of work. The question you're undoubtedly facing now is: "How do I showcase years of education, achievements and outside interests on a CV?" There is no simple answer. Every CV is unique and needs to be tailored for each industry and company, so this is where your research needs to begin.

Recent research from the *National Citizen Service (NCS)* shows that employers have less and less time to review entry level CVs. On average you have just 8.8 seconds to stand out, so you need to be able to sell yourself and your strengths quickly.

First, study the company you're targeting. Have a look at their mission statement if it's online. Use any insight into the company and the role you're applying for to highlight how your skills and attributes would fit with the company you're applying to.

Numbers and percentages are always easy to digest quickly on a CV. If you can clearly show statistics that showcase your achievements then do so, but never exaggerate or embellish the truth. […]

You may think it can be difficult to stand out, but you just need to add [a] touch of personality. I always look for that something extra, something which shows your personal drive and ambition.

In an increasingly competitive job market, graduate recruits need to be able to demonstrate they have something more to offer than just academic performance. High grades don't guarantee a job or even an interview. The study by *NCS* goes on to reveal that half of employers would actually dismiss a CV if the candidate wasn't able to demonstrate experiences outside of the education system.

Highlight the work you have done outside school to show you're not afraid to put in the extra work for something you believe in. Academic qualifications are great to put on a CV and are incredibly important, but life experiences and extracurricular activities speak volumes about your character, not just your intelligence. An employer is looking for someone who can not only get the job done, but someone who will fit within the culture of their organisation and get along with the team already in place. One example is to list any youth programmes you've participated in, any volunteering experiences, passion projects or sport and social activities that you actively pursue. [...]

While you're writing your CV, keep asking yourself what you want this employer to know about you – what personal skills you are most proud of and how you could be an asset to their business. List specific skills that you have, such as confidence and resilience, presenting skills, the ability to work effectively in teams or examples of leading one. These traits are often neglected in CVs yet they are vital for the workplace. [...] You may have heard the advice that you should imitate your interviewer's movements and gestures as a technique to get them to trust you – the same can be said for CVs. Read the job description and copy the language they use. This will show that you not only read their brief fully, but you can use language that resonates with them. [...]

Last but not least, we can often focus so much on making sure the content is right, that we forget the most obvious of rules. Your CV needs to look good as well as sound good. The top three things that turn off employers is bad grammar, spelling mistakes and poor formatting. Take advantage of simple online templates or even use your own creativity – just remember to have a fresh pair of eyes look at it before you send it out.

There's nothing to be afraid of when writing your first CV – it is ultimately all about you, and you know yourself best. If you get through to an interview my best advice is to be professional but more importantly be yourself. Enthusiasm and a keenness to learn are always attractive. Everyone knows a story about a person with the perfect grades that didn't get the job because they lacked personality, so make sure you bring that to the table too.

(699 words)

Quelle: Piers Linney, *The Guardian*, 4 February 2015.

a) Read the article from *The Guardian* and complete the sentences with information from the text.

1. Keep in mind that every CV is unique so the information you give in your CV depends on ______________________________.
2. Employers usually only take ______________________________ to look at your CV.
3. When doing research on the company you want to apply to look out for ______________________________.
4. You should not only list your general skills and attributes but you should ______________________________.
5. Many employers do not only look for high grades but they also ______________________________.
6. Examples of life experiences and extracurricular activities that you could mention in your CV are ______________________________.
7. Another important aspect of your CV are personal skills, for example ______________________________.
8. The three things that make employers stop reading your CV are ______________________________.

9. When you only have poor computer skills you can ____.

10. The most important aspect to keep in mind when writing your CV is that you ____.

b) **Do the following tasks in complete sentences.**

1. Give reasons why it is important to put reasonable effort into writing a CV according to the text.
2. Outline the eight tips given by the author.
3. Explain why it is important to offer more than just academic performance according to the text.

c) **Using your own words summarize the main ideas of the text. Write about 250 words.**

B | Mediation

3 English – German

You have read the following article from *The Guardian* about how hard it is to decide whether to take a gap year or not. You want to tell your friends about the pros and cons of taking a gap year in German.

The big decision: should I take a gap year?

It may not be for everyone, but taking a year out can help you gain valuable experience – and even make you change course.

When I applied to university I thought seriously about taking a gap year. After a year at college, I was utterly demoralised. I hated the early mornings, and felt that I wouldn't have the motivation to attend university. I felt the best course of action would be to defer my application and have a year of saving up, hopefully gaining more work experience – and maybe even fit in some travelling. […]

In the end, I decided against taking a gap year – I wanted to study English literature, and thought a year out would mean my essay practice would diminish. I also knew that I could still keep my job at my local newspaper and my part-time job while I was there.

Weighing up all the options, a gap year no longer seemed relevant.

The idea of spending a year away from home is something that appeals to nearly everyone. So why is taking a gap year still considered the wildcard? "We saw a presentation on taking gap years at college", says college student Holly Brooks. "But none of my friends fancied it, and I didn't want to do it alone, especially considering the expense over the course of a year."

For a teenage student, the prospect of providing for yourself, miles away from home, can be daunting. This is the primary reason many give for not ticking the deferred entry option box and booking the round-the-world plane ticket. […]

Gap years aren't for everyone. Readjusting to an academic timetable after spending time abroad can be a shock. You also need to consider the practicalities, from financing your gap year to surviving without home comforts. […]

(306 words)

Quelle: Helen Whitehouse, *The Guardian*, 27 June 2013.

4 German – English

Sie möchten Ihren englischsprachigen E-Mail-Freund in Spanien über die Möglichkeiten eines Gap-Year informieren. Dafür haben Sie den Text „Was mache ich im Gap-Year?" auf der Homepage der Zeitung *Die Zeit* gefunden. Notieren Sie die wichtigsten Fakten in Stichpunkten auf Englisch.

Gap-Year-Programme

Das Gap-Year wird […] immer populärer und gehört in vielen angelsächsischen Ländern selbstverständlich in die Lebensplanung. […]

Sprachreisen

Sprachreisen können in Großstädte wie London oder New York führen, an die Strände von Barcelona, Miami oder Honolulu oder für den Arabischkurs in den Oman. Es gibt Kurse, bei denen die Unterkunft im Internat oder College angeboten wird. Man kann aber auch in einem Hotel, bei einer Gastfamilie oder in einer WG wohnen. Die Kosten variieren sehr stark, je nachdem, ob man eine Reise von zwei, drei Wochen oder drei Monaten plant oder gar ein Multi-Language-Year machen möchte. […]

„Work and Travel"

Als Au-pair in einer französischen Gastfamilie arbeiten oder in einem Hostel in Kanada aushelfen. So etwas lässt sich mit dem *„Work and Travel"*-Programm umsetzen. Altersbegrenzungen muss man bei den jeweiligen Botschaften erfragen.

Freiwilligendienste

Zum Angebot der *„Work and Travel"*-Agenturen zählen auch Freiwilligendienste. So kann man zum Beispiel eine Nichtregierungsorganisation in einem ghanaischen Dorf bei der HIV-Prävention unterstützen. […] Die Organisation *WWOOF (World-Wide Opportunities on Organic Farms)* vermittelt Aufenthalte auf Bauernhöfen in vielen Teilen der Welt. „Wwoofer" arbeiten gegen Kost und Logis auf den Höfen mit.

Berufserfahrung

Für ein Auslandspraktikum kann man deutsche, international aufgestellte Unternehmen fragen, ob eine Hospitanz in einer Auslandsvertretung möglich ist. Es gibt auch spezialisierte Agenturen, die Praktika vermitteln. […] Auch die Arbeitsagentur bietet in der Auslands- und Fachvermittlung Job- und Praktikumsmöglichkeiten im Ausland an. Oder warum nicht Berufserfahrung als Ski-, Snowboard- oder Tauchlehrer sammeln?

(234 Wörter)

Quelle: Silke Weber, *Zeit Campus Ratgeber*, 26. September 2015.

C | Production

5 Advertisement

Describe and analyze the following advertisement.

6 Composition

For some years now there has been a lot of discussion about the possibilities young people have after finishing school. Discuss the advantages and possible disadvantages of taking a gap year and state your point of view.

D | Business communication

7 Enquiry

Write the following enquiry in English.

Situation: Sie arbeiten für die *Berlin-Handel GmbH*, einem deutschen Importeur von Nonfood-Produkten, und Sie sind auf der Suche nach günstigen Angeboten auf dem asiatischen Markt. Ihre Kunden sind Supermarktketten, die Interesse an Werbegeschenken *(giveaways)* für Werbemaßnahmen haben.

Aufgabe: Sie haben die folgende Homepage gefunden und schreiben eine E-Mail an das chinesische Unternehmen, in der Sie sich nach möglichen interessanten Produkten erkundigen. Sie wünschen Informationen über Preise, Rabatte, Liefer- und Zahlungsbedingungen sowie die Lieferzeiten.

http://www. . . . .cn

TopTen Gift Limited

Home | **Company Info** | Product List | Special Offers | Contact

Founded by a young and energetic group, with more than 10 years of experience in the industry and service excellence, Ningbo *TopTen Gift Limited* is one of the leading producers and exporters in the promotion gifts area.

Our goal is to make you one of our regular customers.

We are proud to offer a wide selection of promotional products, advertising gifts, trade show giveaways, imprints to specification ...

Just some examples of our range:

Contact details:

Company Name	TopTen Gift Limited
Company Address	Room 404, No. 31, Lane 89, Guofeng Street, Haishu, Ningbo, Zhejiang, China
Zip/Postal Code	315040
Telephone Number	86-574-81950391
Fax Number	86-574-87245431
Contact Person	Ms Sony Sung
E-mail Address	sony.sung@topten.gift.china.com

Unit 17

Modern media and marketing

A | Reception

1 Listening comprehension

A 3.16

You are going to hear an extract from a lecture at an English university which talks about the effects of mass media on children and teenagers. Listen to the lecture and complete the following sentences.

1. The advertising industry in particular uses the media to address teenagers because ______________________________.
2. The music industry targets teenagers because ______________________________.
3. Advertising in the media can have a bad influence on teenagers by ______________________________.
4. The professor gives one example of a company that promotes positive messages. They ______________________________.
5. Governments can also help to protect young people by ______________________________.

2 Reading comprehension

Teens' night-time use of social media 'risks harming mental health'

Teenagers who engage with social media during the night could be damaging their sleep and increasing their risk of depression and anxiety, research shows.

More than 460 teenagers at a secondary school in Scotland were questioned about their general social media habits, and in particular their night-time use of sites such as *Facebook* and *Twitter*, as part of the study by Glasgow University.

It found that while overall use of social media affects the quality of sleep, those who log on at night to respond to alerts are particularly affected. It remains unclear, however, whether it is social media that is damaging sleep, or whether teenagers turn to social media because they can't sleep for some other reason.

Dr Heather Cleland Woods said her study had found that children as young as 11 were on

Facebook and *Twitter* and using them considerably. Some pupils at the Glasgow school were using multiple devices – a phone and a tablet for example – to view multiple sites simultaneously and were on them "into the early hours of the morning".

Cleland Woods, who presented the paper at a *British Psychological Society* conference in Manchester on Friday, said: "Adolescence can be a period of increased vulnerability for the onset of depression and anxiety, and poor sleep quality may contribute to this."

"It is important that we understand how social media use relates to these. Evidence is increasingly supporting a link between social media use and wellbeing, particularly during adolescence, but the causes of this are unclear."

She continued: "While overall social media use impacts on sleep quality, those who log on at night appear to be particularly affected. This may be mostly true of individuals who are highly emotionally invested. This means we have to think about how our kids use social media, in relation to time for switching off."

Cleland Woods, a mother of two whose background is in sleep research, posed the idea of a "digital sunset": in the same way that the sun sets a couple of hours before bed, we do the same with our digital devices before bedtime to potentially improve sleep.

As well as being asked about their social media habits, the pupils, aged between 11 and 17, were also asked to respond to a questionnaire which measured sleep quality, self-esteem, anxiety and depression. They were also asked about their emotional investment in social media, the pressure they felt to be available 24/7, and the resulting anxiety if they did not respond immediately to texts or posts.

Preliminary analysis of the research showed overall social media use, and specifically night-time use, was related to poorer sleep quality, lower self-esteem and higher levels of anxiety and depression. A pronounced emotional investment in social media had a similar effect.

Separately, a study of teenage stress commissioned by the *National Citizen's Service* youth programme suggests that girls seek comfort from social media when they are anxious and worried.

The survey of 1,000 12–18-year-olds found that nine out of 10 teenage girls have experienced stress in the past year, with seven in 10 cases leading to symptoms of stress-related illnesses. Rather than talking to their parents, girls are more likely to turn to social media, distracting themselves from the pressure they're under by Snapchatting friends or browsing *Facebook*.

The survey suggests that girls are likely to experience stress more frequently than boys, and more often than the average adult, with girls feeling stressed an average of twice a week. The cause of stress, the survey suggests, is increasingly the anxiety of making important life decisions, with many teenagers suffering from decision paralysis. It found the top three sources of stress for girls were exam results (57 %), making decisions about the future (37 %) and arguments with friends (36 %).

Lucie Russell, campaigns director at the youth mental health charity *Young Minds*, said: "We should not underestimate the huge amount of pressure young people are facing, especially at this time of year which brings the uncertainties that come with a new academic year.

"Not only has social media added new complexities to their daily lives, but looming, uncertain futures just add to this stress. We need to ensure young people are equipped with the skills to deal with these pressures and to navigate positive paths into adulthood."

(720 words)

Quelle: Sally Weale, *The Guardian*, 11 September 2015.

a) Read the newspaper article from *The Guardian* and decide which of the statements are true according to the text. More than one option may be correct.

1. The newspaper article presents the findings of …
   a) a Scottish survey involving a group of teenagers. ☐
   b) a Scottish survey involving students at Glasgow University. ☐
   c) overall social media routines among teenagers. ☐
   d) teenagers' use of social networking sites during the night. ☐

2. The researchers found out that …
   a) the total use of social media affects the quality of sleep. ☐
   b) the night-time use of social media does not affect the quality of sleep. ☐
   c) teenagers turn to social media because they can't sleep. ☐
   d) 11-year-olds do not often use *Facebook* and *Twitter*. ☐

3. The research results show that …
   a) poor sleep quality generally leads to depression and anxiety.
   b) poor sleep quality can contribute to mental health problems.
   c) social media use and health are linked.
   d) the reasons for a growing use of social media are obvious.

4. As a solution the author suggests …
   a) banning digital devices from the bedroom before sunset.
   b) introducing a digital sunset and switching off digital devices before going to bed.
   c) going to bed after sunset.
   d) providing teenagers with skills to handle pressures.

5. The study by the *National Citizen's Service* youth programme found out that …
   a) 90 percent of teenage girls have experienced stress.
   b) teenage girls are as stressed as teenage boys because of their exam results.
   c) 70 percent of teenage girls show symptoms of illnesses that can be related to stress.
   d) girls more often turn to social media when they want to talk instead of turning to their parents.

b) Do the following tasks on the text in complete sentences.

1. Describe the topics that researchers asked students about at a secondary school in Scotland.
2. Explain what the researchers found out.
3. Outline the effect of poor sleep quality according to Cleland Woods.
4. Present the research results of the *National Citizen's Service* youth programme.

c) Using your own words summarize the main ideas of the text. The summary should be about 250 words long.

B | Mediation

3 English – German

You have read the article from *The Guardian* about alcohol advertising targeted at teenagers on *Facebook* and you want to tell your classmates about the dangers of this type of advertising in German.

Facebook deal with *Diageo* fuels under-age drinking fears

Drinks giant's marketing tie-up on advertising pages raises concerns about health impact on teenagers.

A multimillion-dollar deal agreed between *Facebook* and drinks company *Diageo* will fuel the under-age drinking epidemic by exposing increasing numbers of young people to alcohol marketing, health experts are warning.

[…] Health experts and alcohol campaigners say the impact will be felt in teenage drinking.

Dr Nick Sheron, a liver specialist at Southampton hospital, is one of those who believes the attraction of *Facebook* is the youth of its users, with half under the age of 24 and many under the legal drinking age of 18.

Facebook argues that pages set up by alcohol advertisers are "age-gated", and therefore only accessible to those who are over 18. But Sheron argues that many younger people do not disclose their true age on *Facebook*.

"The age verification process for social networking sites is clearly completely ineffective – even though users are supposed to be 13 or above, it has been suggested that one-quarter of UK children aged 8–12 have a *Facebook* or similar account," he said

"Secondly, the majority of these accounts are hidden from parents, so *Diageo* effectively has a private narrowcast channel of communication with young people, which it will use to promote alcohol use as a positive lifestyle." [...]

Facebook said it was very hard to control the age group who access any internet site, but insisted that it does all it can. [...]

"It shouldn't be forgotten that making sure services are age-appropriate isn't an issue that is confined to *Facebook* – teens and young people use the wider internet every day, often accessing websites and online services that offer few or no safety tools. We feel that the best solution to using services in an age-appropriate way is for service providers like *Facebook* to carry on working with parents, safety experts and kids themselves to aid education and understanding."

(322 words)

Quelle: Sarah Boseley, *The Guardian*, 20 September 2011.

4 German – English

Sie möchten Ihrem englischsprachigen Freund in Barcelona eine E-Mail schreiben über die Auswirkungen von TV-Werbung für alkoholische Getränke auf das sogenannte Rauschtrinken bei Jugendlichen. Dazu haben Sie auf der Internetseite des Fernsehsenders *N-TV* folgenden Text über die Langzeitstudie einer Krankenkasse gefunden. Notieren Sie die wichtigsten Ergebnisse der Studie für Ihre E-Mail auf Englisch.

TV-Werbung für Alkohol verführt Jugendliche

[...] Alkoholwerbung im Fernsehen verführt Kinder und Jugendliche nach einer Studie von Kieler Wissenschaftlern zum Rauschtrinken. Das häufige Sehen von TV-Werbespots erhöhe das Risiko des sogenannten Komasaufens bis zu viermal. [...]

Bei den Befragten, die am wenigsten Werbung mit Alkohol sahen, hatten der Studie zufolge 6,2 Prozent mehr als fünf Rauscherlebnisse in dem Befragungszeitraum. Bei den Teilnehmern, die am häufigsten TV-Spots für Bier, Wein und Schnaps gesehen hatten, lag die Rauschquote bei 24 Prozent und damit viermal so hoch.

Die Langzeituntersuchung bestätigt nach Angabe der *DAK-Gesundheit* zudem, dass ein riskanter Alkoholkonsum ein verbreitetes Phänomen in Deutschland ist. Die Hälfte der teilnehmenden Schüler habe über ein erstmaliges Rauschtrinken – das sind mindestens fünf alkoholische Getränke bei einer Gelegenheit – innerhalb von 30 Monaten berichtet. 11 Prozent der Mädchen und 18 Prozent der Jungen gaben an, sie hätten sogar mehr als fünf Erfahrungen mit derartig massivem Alkoholkonsum. [...]

„Unsere Studie zeigt, dass Alkoholwerbung von Jugendlichen nicht nur wahrgenommen wird", erklärte der Suchtexperte der *DAK-Gesundheit*, Ralf Kremer. „Die Werbung kann vielmehr als unabhängiger Risikofaktor für die Initiierung des häufigen Rauschtrinkens im Jugendalter angesehen werden." Die Krankenkasse und das *IFT-Nord*, die seit sechs Jahren auch eine gemeinsame Anti-Alkohol-Kampagne betreiben, plädierten für Werbeverbote und die Erziehung der Kinder zu einem kritischen Umgang mit den Werbespots.

(215 Wörter)

Quelle: *N-TV*, 06. Oktober 2015.

C | Production

5 Advertisement

Describe and analyze this advertisement for an alcoholic drink.

6 Composition

For some years now there has been a discussion about the effects of advertising on young people. Discuss the statement "Alcohol advertising should be banned or restricted on TV and the Internet".

D | Business communication

7 Offer

Write the following offer in English.

Situation: Sie arbeiten für die *DERGO Maschinenbau AG* in der Sutterstr. 22 in 33617 Bielefeld (E-Mail-Adresse: name@dergo-maschinen.de), ein mittlerweile über 100 Jahre bestehendes Unternehmen, das sich auf die Herstellung von CNC-Maschinen für die Metallbearbeitung spezialisiert hat und Kunden in über 30 Ländern hat. Sie haben eine Anfrage von Obama Tutu (E-Mail-Adresse: tutu@southteco.com) von der Firma *Southteco* in Cape Town 8001 in Südafrika, 36 Mandela Road, bekommen, in der sich das Unternehmen nach den neuesten CNC-Maschinen erkundigt.

Aufgabe: Schreiben Sie per E-Mail oder Brief ein Angebot an Herrn Tutu.
- Bedanken Sie sich für die Anfrage vom ...
- Stellen Sie kurz Ihr Unternehmen vor.
- Erwähnen Sie Ihre langjährige Erfahrung und den hohen technischen Standard Ihrer Produkte.
- Weisen Sie auf Ihre neueste Entwicklung hin: CNC-Dreh- und Fräszentrum *(lathe and milling centre)* LMC02.
- Betonen Sie, dass diese Maschine sich durch eine einfache Bedienung und hohe Präzision auszeichnet.
- Weisen Sie auf die Preisliste hin, die Sie als Anlage mitschicken, und auf den Online-Katalog mit Ihrem umfangreichen Angebot auf der Unternehmenswebsite.
- Nennen Sie als Zahlungsbedingungen die Zahlung per Akkreditiv.
- Geben Sie als Lieferungsbedingung FOB Rotterdam an.
- Bedanken Sie sich noch einmal höflich für das Interesse und bekunden Sie Ihren Wunsch, mit dem südafrikanischen Unternehmen in Geschäftsbeziehungen zu treten.

Unit 18

Money makes the world go round

A | Reception

1 Listening comprehension

A 3.17

Lately there has been a discussion about young adults and students who have serious financial problems. Listen to the radio interview in which two students and an expert from the *Citizens Advice Bureau* in Southampton talk about student debt. Decide which of the statements are true. More than one option may be correct.

1. Debbie and Kieran have got into financial difficulties because they…
   a) wanted to have more free-time. ☐
   b) are preparing for their final exams. ☐
   c) were only working part-time. ☐
   d) had to quit their part-time jobs. ☐
2. Last year Debbie and Kieran went on a holiday trip and …
   a) booked a cheap ferry to Ibiza. ☐
   b) booked an expensive hotel room in a holiday resort on the island of Ibiza. ☐
   c) found accommodation in a rather inexpensive hotel. ☐
   d) realized that a holiday on Ibiza is not cheap. ☐
3. When Debbie and Kieran got back to Southampton they …
   a) were quite relaxed. ☐
   b) noticed that they had spent too much money on Ibiza. ☐
   c) had problems paying for their running costs. ☐
   d) noticed that their credit cards had been stolen. ☐
4. Mike Rowling points out that after their graduation students …
   a) owe 2,000 pounds on average. ☐
   b) owe about 10,000 pounds in student loans on average. ☐
   c) usually need to pay back money to their families. ☐
   d) do not have to pay back bank loans. ☐
5. Mike Rowling advises students to …
   a) check out their financial problems. ☐
   b) make a debts list and an expenses list. ☐
   c) pay back their debts immediately. ☐
   d) spend more money. ☐

2 Reading comprehension

Prom night can cost teenagers (and parents) a pretty penny

On average, US families are spending as much as $ 919 on their teen's prom expenses

Prom, for Brianna Albert, was an experience she will never forget – and not just because two of her classmates got into a fight over wearing the same dress. While she has fond memories of last year's "night to remember", she remembers the cost and the stress too.

Many US teenagers and parents are feeling those same stresses now as prom season gets into full swing again. A recent survey from *Visa* showed that the average US family plans to spend about $ 919 on a prom-going teen, with parents covering as much as 73 % of the costs. [...]

Albert said that her parents – a preschool teacher and a lawyer – paid for the dress, her hair and her share of the costs of a limo rental. "My dress was relatively inexpensive. Luckily, it was only $ 80. I actually didn't even find my dress [...]," she said, explaining that her mom bought it while on a trip to Boston. [...]

With this year's proms just weeks away, teenagers at high schools across the US are already racking up hundreds of dollars in prom-related expenses. [...]

Families with lower incomes spend the most, according to the *Visa* survey. Families with income below $ 25,000 planned to spend $ 1,393 while families with income below $ 50,000 planned to spend $ 1,109 and families with income over $ 50,000 planned to spend an average of $ 799.

"I can't really imagine spending $ 1,000 on prom myself," said Morgan [high school student]. "If someone did, they might [hire] a limo, professional photographer with professional lighting – apparently that's a thing – and buy a really fancy dress, expensive flowers like orchids, fancy dinner, etc."

There are others, however, who could easily find a way to spend a $ 1,000. "I can definitely see myself spending $ 1,000 on prom. Last year, since I went to two proms, I spent around $ 900," Esther Galo, 18, told the *Guardian*. [...]

Galo said that her mom, who works as a nurse, paid for all of her prom expenses. To get the best deal on items like makeup, tanning and limo, they looked to *Groupon* or *Living Social* for discounts. [...]

Promposals

It's not just the girls who begin planning and spending money months beforehand.

"It's no longer acceptable to just 'ask' a girl to prom," Ashleigh Prendable, a teacher at Albert's school, the Colonel Zadok Magruder high school in Gaithersburg, Maryland, told the *Guardian*.

As a result, promposals – elaborate invitations to proms – are setting some US teenagers back by as much as $ 324, according to *Visa's* survey.

Prendable's students have devised scavenger hunts, flashmobs, and even built their prom proposals into lesson plans. One student got a math teacher to devise a problem with the variables P, R and M – instead of the usual X, Y and Z – and the number 0. [...]

No teen left behind

To make sure that underprivileged students are not left out of the end-of-the-year activities, nonprofits like *Operation Prom* and *Cinderella* and *Prince Charming Project* are providing low-income students with free formal wear.

"Senior year is a tough year," Noel D'Allacco, founder of *Operation Prom*, told *CNN*. "You already have to think about the costs for college so then tacking on the price tag of the dress, the tuxedo rental, the prom tickets, the limo, the flowers, the hair, the makeup, everything that you need, you are looking at a lot of money that families and the students are worried about that senior year." [...]

While the teens are excited for their upcoming proms, they insist that the night is "really not a huge deal".

"It's weird because it's expected to be this huge thing, so you spend all this money on it, but many at my school would agree that it's not the end-all-be-all that it once was," said Morgan. [...]

Galo, on the other hand, believes that spending money on prom is a worthy investment.

"For me, since prom only happens twice in your life, it is worth investing in it. You want to look back on pictures and remember the fun you had and how it was a night you felt and looked your best," she said. "The memories you make will last forever, so you want to make sure they're good ones!"

(726 words)

Quelle: Jana Kasperkevic, *The Guardian*, 20 April 2015.

a) **Read the newspaper article from *The Guardian* and complete the following sentences with information from the text.**

1. For the average American family the expenses for a prom night add up to ______________________.
2. When Brianna Albert remembers her prom she thinks on the one hand of ______________________ and on the other hand of ______________________.
3. On average parents only pay ______________________.
4. Esther Galo says that they were looking on websites like ______________________ for ______________________.
5. While girls spend money on ______________________ boys spend money on ______________________.
6. Low-income families will be supported with ______________________ by ______________________.
7. Although teenagers are spending huge amounts of money on prom night they think ______________________ ______________________.

b) **Do the following tasks in complete sentences.**

1. Outline the findings of the survey by *Visa*.
2. Describe what things the teenagers spend money on when getting ready for their prom night.
3. Explain what "promposals" are according to the text.
4. Contrast the positive and negative sides of prom nights as mentioned in the text.

c) **Using your own words summarize the main ideas of the text. Write about 250 words.**

B | Mediation

3 English – German

You have read the following article from *The Guardian* about the unfair payment of sportswomen and you want to tell your teammates about the main aspects in German.

Female sport stars should earn the same as their male counterparts

[…] I remember picking up my first winner's cheque of €500 at a small competition in Ireland and thinking I had made it. Until I realised that men in the 100m at the same event received €2,000. It was a rude awakening.

Although many sports have moved into the 21st century and award equal prize money at major competitions, 30 % of sports, including football, cricket and squash, refuse to move forward, as was highlighted this week in a study by the *BBC*. […]

It has been argued that women's sport isn't as businesslike as men's, that it doesn't generate enough interest to justify equality on the pay scale. But this is because they refuse to give women's sport the same platform. Many of the sports that offer equal pay also allow both men and women the chance to share a platform: athletics, cycling, skating and swimming have world championships that both genders are able to participate in. […]

I was always cautious when discussing how much money I would make from sport, especially surrounding sponsorship contracts. I had seen proof that I wasn't getting the best deal and suspected that it wasn't based on performance, but rather my gender. Young male sprinters would receive more media attention and more money, having not achieved the levels I had reached. [...]

It wasn't until three substandard kit contracts later in my career that I realised just because you are living your dream, it doesn't mean you can't want more from it financially.

(260 words)

Quelle: Jeanette Kwakye, *The Guardian*, 31 October 2014.

4 German – English

Sie möchten im Rahmen Ihres Austauschjahres in England einen Vortrag über Sponsoring im Sport halten. Dafür haben Sie den Text aus dem *Tagesspiegel* über die Ausprägungen von Sponsorendeals im Profisport gefunden. Notieren Sie die wichtigsten Fakten für Ihren Vortrag auf Englisch.

Her mit dem Geld!

[...] Eine Viertelmilliarde US Dollar ist eine Menge Geld. Vor allem, wenn man es dafür erhält, ein kleines Logo auf dem Hemd zu tragen und den Golfschlager zu wechseln. Umgerechnet knapp 200 Millionen Euro soll der Sportartikelhersteller *Nike* dem Golfer Rory McIlroy bieten, damit er die nächsten zehn Jahre das Häkchenlogo spazieren trägt. Wird der von amerikanischen Medien vermeldete Deal offiziell bestätigt, dann stellt der 23-jährige Nordire einen neuen Sponsoringrekord im Sport auf. [...]

Der neue Rekord lässt Fragen über den Sinn und Unsinn des Sponsorings von Sportlern aufkommen. Seit Anbeginn des Profitums unter Athleten gang und gäbe, investieren Unternehmen Unsummen nicht nur in Klubs und Mannschaften, deren Fortbestand, Popularität und teils auch Erfolg zumindest annähernd sicher ist, sondern auch in Sportler, deren Karriere jeden Moment vorbei sein könnte.

Dem Risiko zum Trotz, sagt Pascal Schulte vom Branchen-Analysten „*Sport+Markt*": „Der Vertrag macht aus Sicht von *Nike* durchaus Sinn. Golf ist vor allem in den englischsprachigen Ländern sehr beliebt, dort wird es sogar in Kneipen übertragen." Vor allem der US-Riese *Nike* ist immer wieder für rekordverdächtige Sponsorendeals gut, denn sie haben den Konzern zur Weltmarke gemacht. [...]

Mancher Profi veränderte für einen Sponsorenvertrag sogar sein Äußeres. Paul Breitner, wegen seiner Afrofrisur und seinem nicht gerade latent zur Schau gestellten Interesse am Kommunismus als „Revoluzzer" betitelt, trug viele Jahre einen prächtigen Vollbart. Kurz vor der Fußball-Weltmeisterschaft 1982 schor der Nationalspieler den Bart ab und warb für einen Rasierwasser-Hersteller, dem dieser Coup 150.000 Mark wert war.

Zuweilen werben Sportler auch für Dinge, mit denen sie sich weniger identifizieren konnten oder nach eigener Aussage keine Verwendung dafür hatten. Pelé, Brasiliens Fußball-Idol, warb vor einigen Jahren für die Potenzpille *Viagra*, wurde aber nicht müde zu betonen, das Produkt nie genommen zu haben. [...]

Nach den guten Erfahrungen mit Tiger Woods will *Nike* McIlroy als neues Gesicht der Marke aufbauen. „Für einen 23-Jährigen ist McIlroy schon sehr weit, er kann der Golf-Superstar der nächsten Jahre werden", sagt Schulte. Denn Woods' Image hat trotz des sportlich erfolgreichen Comebacks Schaden genommen durch private Eskapaden. Von Lance Armstrong trennte sich das Unternehmen wegen dessen Dopingskandal. [...]

(344 Wörter)

Quelle: Dominik Bardow und Sebastian Stier, *Der Tagesspiegel*, 10. Januar 2013.

C | Production

5 Cartoon

Describe and analyze the cartoon on the right.

6 Diagram

Describe and analyze the following diagram.

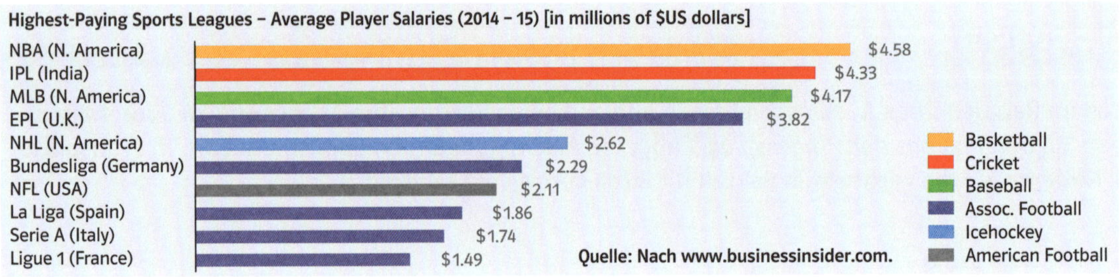

7 Composition

For some years now there has been a discussion about the effects of money on international sport. Discuss the influence of money on sports and state your point of view.

D | Business communication

8 Order

Write the following order in English.

Situation: Sie arbeiten im Einkauf der *Schumann Freizeit GmbH*, Maxstraße 11 in 30169 Hannover, Tel. +44(0)511 5432842, E-Mail: name@schumann.de. Sie haben ein Angebot von Claire Winter, tätig in der Exportabteilung des britischen Unternehmens *Toys World Unlimited*, 22 Bridge Road, Bath BA 1 1BX, bekommen.

Aufgabe: Schreiben Sie mit heutigem Datum eine Bestellung per E-Mail oder Brief an *Toys World Unlimited*.
- Bedanken Sie sich für das interessante Angebot.
- Bestellen Sie 5.000 Dartboards mit der Bestellnummer DG341 zum Preis von 17, 75 £ pro Stück.
- Da es sich um einen Erstauftrag handelt, erwarten Sie einen Einführungsrabatt von 10 %.
- Sie wiederholen die Zahlungsbedingungen: 50 % der Rechnungssumme werden im Voraus bezahlt, der Rest wird innerhalb von 30 Tagen nach Lieferung überwiesen.
- Die Lieferung soll innerhalb von vier Wochen per LKW erfolgen.
- Sie bitten um eine umgehende Bestätigung dieses Auftrags.
- Da Sie die Ware dringend benötigen, bitten Sie um Nachricht, falls es zu Lieferungsverzögerungen kommt.
- Bekunden Sie Ihre Freude, mit dem britischen Unternehmen in Zukunft Geschäfte zu machen.

Unit 19

Technological developments and environment

A | Reception

1 Listening comprehension

A 3.18

Every two years the *European Union* hosts the European Climate Change Adaptation Conference. The conference offers a platform to present and discuss new technologies which help to stop climate change. Listen to two experts as they talk about current research projects in their companies and answer the following questions.

1. What product is the company *Severn Soft Cells* developing at the present time? ____________________
2. How does *Severn Soft Cells'* newest product work?
____
____
3. What will the advantages of this product be?
____
____
4. According to John Skinner, what happens with ordinary household batteries when they are empty?
____
____
5. How does *RecycleMore's* product differ from traditional products which are already on the market?
____
____

2 Reading comprehension

Why the modern world is bad for your brain

[…] Our brains are busier than ever before. We're assaulted with facts, pseudo facts, jibber-jabber, and rumour, all posing as information. Trying to figure out what you need to know and what you can ignore is exhausting. At the same time, we are all doing more. Thirty years ago, travel agents made our airline and rail reservations, salespeople helped us find what we were looking for in shops, and professional typists or secretaries helped busy people with their correspondence. Now we do most of those things ourselves. We are doing the jobs of 10 different people while still trying to keep up with our lives, our children and parents, our friends, our careers, our hobbies, and our favourite TV shows.

Our smartphones have become Swiss army knife-like appliances that include a dictionary, calculator, web browser, email, *Game Boy*, appointment calendar, voice recorder, guitar tuner, weather forecaster, GPS, texter, tweeter, *Facebook* updater, and flashlight. They're more powerful and do more things than the most advanced computer at *IBM* corporate head-quarters 30 years ago. And we use them all the time, part of a 21st-century mania for cramming everything we do into every single spare moment of downtime. We text while we're walking across the street, catch up on email while standing in a queue – and while having lunch with friends, we surreptitiously check to see what our other friends are doing. [...]

But there's a fly in the ointment. Although we think we're doing several things at once, multitasking, this is a powerful and diabolical illusion. Earl Miller, a neuroscientist at *MIT* and one of the world experts on divided attention, says that our brains are "not wired to multitask well... When people think they're multitasking, they're actually just switching from one task to another very rapidly. And every time they do, there's a cognitive cost in doing so." [...] Even though we think we're getting a lot done, ironically, multitasking makes us demonstrably less efficient. Multitasking has been found to increase the production of the stress hormone cortisol as well as the fight-or-flight hormone adrenaline, which can overstimulate your brain and cause mental fog or scrambled thinking. [...]

In the old days, if the phone rang and we were busy, we either didn't answer or we turned the ringer off. When all phones were wired to a wall, there was no expectation of being able to reach us at all times – one might have gone out for a walk or been between places – and so if someone couldn't reach you (or you didn't feel like being reached), it was considered normal. Now more people have mobile phones than have toilets. This has created an implicit expectation that you should be able to reach someone when it is convenient for you, regardless of whether it is convenient for them. [...]

Glenn Wilson, former visiting professor of psychology at Gresham College, London, calls it infomania. His research found that being in a situation where you are trying to concentrate on a task, and an email is sitting unread in your inbox, can reduce your effective IQ by 10 points. [...]

Russ Poldrack, a neuroscientist at Stanford, found that learning information while multitasking causes the new information to go to the wrong part of the brain. If students study and watch TV at the same time, for example, the information from their schoolwork goes into the striatum, a region specialised for storing new procedures and skills, not facts and ideas. Without the distraction of TV, the information goes into the hippocampus, where it is organised and categorised in a variety of ways, making it easier to retrieve. [...]

In discussing information overload with *Fortune 500* leaders, top scientists, writers, students, and small business owners, email comes up again and again as a problem. It's not a philosophical objection to email itself, it's the mind-numbing number of emails that come in. When the 10-year-old son of my neuroscience colleague Jeff Mogil (head of the Pain Genetics lab at McGill University) was asked what his father does for a living, he responded, "He answers emails." Jeff admitted after some thought that it's not so far from the truth. [...]

Before email, if you wanted to write to someone, you had to invest some effort in it. You'd sit down with pen and paper, or at a typewriter, and care-fully compose a message. [...] Because the very act of writing a note or letter to someone took this many steps, and was spread out over time, we didn't go to the trouble unless we had something important to say. Because of email's immediacy, most of us give little thought to typing up any little thing that pops in our heads and hitting the send button.[...]

(798 words)

Quelle: Daniel J Levitin, *The Guardian*, 18 January 2015.

a) Read the text on pages 109 / 110 and decide if the following statements are true or false according to the text. Correct the false statements. Use a separate sheet of paper.

1. Our brains today must do ...
   a) more work because there is a flood of information. ☐
   b) less work because different people do certain jobs for us. ☐
2. Our smartphones ...
   a) help us to get short breaks. ☐
   b) are equipped with many appliances that can be helpful in our everyday lives. ☐
3. Earl Miller points out that our brains are ...
   a) not able to do many tasks at the same time. ☐
   b) able to quickly switch from one task to another. ☐

4. Multitasking …
   a) is the false belief of our brains that we get different things done at the same time.
   b) makes people work more efficiently.
   c) can lead to confusion.
   d) reduces the production of cortisol and adrenaline.

5. Our usage of telephones has changed enormously.
   a) In the past we had wireless telephones.
   b) In the present time we are expected to be available at any time.

6. The consequence of multitasking is that …
   a) people who can multitask have a higher IQ.
   b) you are able to learn information better and store it better in your brain.
   c) watching TV does not distract you when learning things for school.

b) Do the following tasks in complete sentences.

1. Give reasons why our brains are busier today than in the past.
2. Describe what the author wants to point out when he compares our smartphones to Swiss army knives.
3. Explain why multitasking is an illusion according to Earl Miller.
4. Outline the consequences of multitasking.

c) Using your own words summarize the main ideas of the text. Write about 250 words.

B | Mediation

3 English – German

Sie haben diesen Artikel über gesündere Städte gefunden und möchten die Informationen nutzen, um einen Brief auf Deutsch an den Bürgermeister/ die Bürgermeisterin Ihrer Heimatstadt zu verfassen. Informieren Sie in dem Brief anhand dieses Artikels, welche Gefahren das Leben in den Städten mit sich bringt und stellen Sie dem Bürgermeister/ der Bürgermeisterin auch Projekte vor, die in anderen Städten umgesetzt wurden.

How to create healthier cities

Air quality is deteriorating in many of the world's cities. Nearly two-thirds of people with diabetes live in urban areas. Wealthier lifestyles, prioritising convenience and fast food, have led even formerly famine-stricken China to admit an obesity epidemic. Urban dwellers have far-higher stress levels than their rural counterparts.

If that's city living, who'd do it? Well, 54 % of us and counting. With that much of the world's population living in urban areas, cities surely have a duty to do a better job of protecting public health. It's not only a question of residents' wellbeing: cities with physically active residents are more economically productive than their sedentary counterparts.

Many cities have started to take health seriously. Copenhagen replaced a driving culture with one of walking and cycling. Sydney is stocked with high quality sports clubs and facilities. Singapore's expert grasp of data and technology has led to low-carbon and sustainable models of urban design.

Even Tokyo, the world's biggest city, has one of the world's best public transport systems meaning it keeps greenhouse gas emissions relatively low. And Hong Kong may have an extremely dense population, but its residents often travel on foot and many of them are doctors.

(203 words)

Quelle: Tamsin Rutter, *The Guardian*, 12 October 2015.

4 German – English

Sie haben diesen Artikel über autofreie Städte gefunden und möchten Ihrem E-Mail-Freund in Rom, mit dem Sie auf Englisch korrespondieren, darüber berichten. Informieren Sie Ihren Freund anhand dieses Artikels, welche Vorteile und welche Nachteile autofreie Städte mit sich bringen.

„Autofreie Städte? Wunderbar!“

„Sicher müssen Autos raus aus der Stadt. Ich habe seit 33 Jahren keins mehr“, schreibt der Grünen-Abgeordnete Michael Cramer in der aktuellen Wochenendausgabe der *taz*. Cramer sitzt für die Grünen im Europaparlament und weist darauf hin, dass seine Partei schon 1984 die Idee der autofreien Städte propagiert habe.

„Die Große Koalition wollte daraufhin den Autoanteil auf 20 Prozent senken.“ Und heute? Führe die autofixierte Stadtentwicklungspolitik ins Chaos. Bus und Bahn seien zu teuer, die Parkgebühren dafür zu billig. [...]

Für die Sicherheit der Bürger wäre eine Einschränkung des Verkehrs wohl besser. Mehr als 3.500 Menschen sterben jährlich in Deutschland im Straßenverkehr, insgesamt gab es im Jahr 2010 knapp 2,5 Millionen Unfälle mit motorisierten Fahrzeugen, die volkswirtschaftlichen Kosten betragen laut der Bundesanstalt für Straßenwesen 31 Milliarden Euro.

Also Kraftfahrzeuge verbannen – und alles wird gut? Nein, schreibt die Rennfahrerin Ellen Lohr. Allerdings nicht, weil sie mit ihrem *Lamborghini* unbedingt durch die Stadt rasen will. „Ich habe drei Kinder“, sagt sie. „Jeden, der von einer autofreien Stadt träumt, würde ich gern mit dem *Maxi Cosi* in der Hand zum Kinderarzt schicken, während zwei andere Kids rumnerven.“ Lohr hofft, dass die Zukunft uns eben nicht Ideen wie in London oder Turin beschert, wo die Innenstadt beispielsweise Maut kostet.

Die österreichische Köchin und überzeugte Fußgängerin Sarah Wiener sieht das ganz anders. Sie schreibt: „Autofreie Städte! Wunderbar!“ Wiener glaubt, die Menschen würden so automatisch gesünder, agiler und bewegungsfreudiger. In Italien und Südfrankreich gebe es doch schon autofreie Dörfer und Kleinstädte. Die Erfahrung dort – wie auch in autofreien Stadtteilen in Münster oder Freiburg: Die Lebensqualität steige schlagartig. [...]

Die Fahrradkurierin Anja Rillcke aus Köln hält eine autofreie Stadt für keine so gute Idee. Dann wäre doch der alltägliche Machtkampf – Auto gegen Rad – vorbei.

(289 Wörter)

Quelle: Emilia Smechowski, *TAZ*, 24.03.2012.

C | Production

5 Cartoon

Describe and analyze the cartoon on the right.

“Isn’t it nice to see children cycling to school?”

6 Diagram

Describe and analyze the following chart.

Factors deterring people from buying an electric car or van in 2015

Question: If you were to buy a car or van in the next 12 months, what, if anything, would put you off buying an electric car or van? (Full driving licence holders only)

	2015
Limited choice (not many vehicles to choose from)	6%
Lack of knowledge	13%
Cost	27%
Battery: distance travelled on charge	36%
Recharging	39%
The vehicle: performance, size / practicality, looks	8%
Technology: doesn't work / not proven	8%
Don't know	7%

More than one response allowed, so total can be more than 100%

Quelle: Nach 2015 & 2014 Office for National Statistics Omnibus/Opinion Survey, Table ATT0506, 18 June 2015.

7 Composition

For some years now there has been a discussion about the possibility of banning all cars from our inner cities. Discuss the pros and cons of this suggestion and state your point of view.

D | Business communication

8 Complaint

Write the following complaint in English.

Situation: Sie arbeiten für die *Danubiste KG*, Erich-Greiner-Str. 11 in 42119 Wuppertal. Sie stehen in regelmäßigen Geschäftsbeziehungen zu einem Zulieferer aus England, der *Hodgson Hill Ltd*, 29 Brick Lane in Exeter EX2 4AN. Ihre Ansprechpartnerin ist Frau Tucker. Das englische Unternehmen hat Ihnen wiederholt zuverlässig Teile geliefert. In den letzten Wochen hat es aber Grund zu Klagen gegeben.

Aufgabe: Schreiben Sie unter dem heutigen Datum eine höfliche Mängelrüge an das englische Unternehmen unter Berücksichtigung der Formvorschriften. Gehen Sie dabei insbesondere auf die folgenden Punkte ein:

- Bereits vor einigen Wochen traf die Lieferung CS 98/12 verspätet ein.
- In der letzten Lieferung CS 98/13 waren 20 Artikel Nr. 342RB beschädigt, möglicherweise wegen unzureichender Verpackung.
- Sie benötigen Ersatz für die beschädigten Artikel innerhalb von zwei Wochen.
- Außerdem möchten Sie wissen, wie Sie mit den beschädigten Produkten verfahren sollen.
- Zudem sind die bestellten Artikel 343RF seit zwei Wochen überfällig, die dringend benötigt werden, um eigene Aufträge ausführen zu können.
- Weisen Sie darauf hin, dass weitere Geschäftsbeziehungen nur möglich sind, wenn in Zukunft der hohe Standard eingehalten wird.
- Ihre Kunden erwarten von Ihnen hohe Qualität und Zuverlässigkeit, deshalb müssen Sie sich auf Ihre Zulieferer verlassen können.
- Beenden Sie den Brief freundlich.

Unit 20

Going global

A | Reception

1 Listening comprehension

A 3.19

Recently there has been a lot of discussion about the consequences of international mass tourism. Listen to two experts and answer the following questions using keywords.

1. How many tourists will be travelling in the next 15 years according to Oliver Parkin?

2. Which two problems will arise as a result of mass tourism according to Parkin?

3. In what way has Manee Luang contributed to making tourism more sustainable?

4. How successful has Manee Luang become?

5. How sustainable is mass tourism really according to Parkin?

2 Reading comprehension

Two years after Rana Plaza, have conditions improved in Bangladesh's factories?

On 24 April 2013, an eight-story garment factory collapsed in Dhaka, the capital of Bangladesh. The building's fall killed 1,134 people and injured hundreds of others. The Rana Plaza tragedy was not caused by an earthquake or a terrorist attack, but rather by poor construction and a lack of oversight – and, in some ways, by a growing global desire for more cheap fashion.

It's been two years since the Rana Plaza tragedy, and although much remains to be done to ensure the rights and safety of workers in Bangladesh's still-booming garment industry, progress has been made. Global brands including

H&M, *Mango*, *Primark*, the *Gap* and *Walmart*, among a dozen others, have contributed $21.5 m to the *Rana Plaza Donors Trust Fund*, which was set up to award compensation to victims and their families. [...]

But the real change will come in the form of improvements to worker safety and worker's rights. According to Reddy [*Anm. Bangladeshi director for the International Labour Organization, ILO*], Dhaka's permitting offices have simply not kept pace with its booming garment industry, leading to a situation in which factories were being given permits without so much as a site visit, much less monitoring.

That has begun to change since the Rana Plaza collapse. According to Reddy, out of 3,508 factories identified as exporting clothing from Bangladesh, almost 75 % have gone through building fire and safety assessments. As a result, 35 factories have been closed for failing to comply with structural integrity standards.

"That is not good news, necessarily, but what's important is to recognize that we might have actually averted some building problems and accidents by closing down these factories," Reddy said, "and putting the remaining factories through the remediation process" that requires building owners to fix various building safety issues. [...]

Several brands and retailers are playing an active role in addressing worker safety issues in Bangladesh, according to Reddy, in terms of both paying for factories to be upgraded and working with government agencies and nongovernmental organizations to draft guidelines and strategies for improving the lot of garment workers.

However, those commitments are set to end in 2018. "So we need to focus on how to continue this work, train monitoring staff, and ensure that capacity is built into the local authorities," Reddy said.

One problem that has yet to be addressed, according to Reddy, is the capacity issue in *Dhaka's Capital Development Authority*. The Authority approves building permits and is supposed to monitor construction to ensure that buildings are built according to the approved design. "Currently they do not really monitor," Reddy said. "They grant permits and then don't monitor, because they just don't have enough monitoring staff. That was one of the problems with Rana Plaza – they were approved for six floors and built eight. That's still a weak link and we're asking the government to step up."

Although the *ILO* and other NGOs are pleased with the progress that has been made on worker safety, worker rights issues have lagged behind. At the end of 2012, there were 122 unions in Bangladesh's garment industry and they represented less than 3 % of workers. [...]

Today there are 437 unions, representing nearly 5 % of workers in the industry. Part of the remediation plans that came out of talks immediately following the Rana Plaza collapse was the need to establish worker safety committees at the city's factories, so that employees would have a place to voice concerns about workplace safety. So far, those committees have not been formed because the government has been slow to draft policies for their creation. [...]

Attention has been good and bad for Bangladesh's garment industry, according to Reddy. On the one hand, it has spurred international brands to take a keen interest in the country, supplying funding, time and ideas to improving the garment industry there. On the other, it has created pressure for the industry to improve rapidly.

"All these issues evolved over the course of the past 30 years, but people wanted to see them fixed in months," Reddy said. "Some people felt like, 'Why is everyone focused on Bangladesh when there are a lot of other exporting countries that don't meet these international standards?'"

The Rana Plaza reforms have not touched 40 % of the country's factories, and these tend to be the facilities that are exporting to various countries through small brands and retailers.

The hope now is that the world will continue to pay attention to these issues, and that smaller companies and brands, not just the big players with reputations to protect, will support reform as well.

(798 words)

Quelle: Amy Westervelt, *The Guardian*, 24 April 2015.

a) Read the text and decide which of the statements are true. More than one option may be correct.

1. The garment factory Rana Plaza in Bangladesh ...
   a) was destroyed when an earthquake hit Dhaka, the capital of Bangladesh. ☐
   b) was a building with eight floors. ☐
   c) collapsed because it was poorly constructed and not checked for safety. ☐
   d) was a fashionable shopping mall in Dhaka, the capital of Bangladesh. ☐

2. After the catastrophe in Dhaka …
   a) they improved the working conditions for workers in the garment industry.
   b) famous brands like *H&M* stopped to produce clothes in Bangladesh.
   c) famous brands like *H&M* paid money to the victims and their families.
   d) the permitting offices have not given any permits for the construction of new factories.

3. Up to the present day they have …
   a) controlled a quarter of Dhaka's garment factory buildings.
   b) inspected three-fourths of Dhaka's garment factories.
   c) won some brands and retailers that put in financial help to upgrade factory buildings.
   d) started to plan guidelines and strategies for the improvement of working conditions in the garment industry in Dhaka.

4. Reddy says that in the future they will …
   a) need to expand local authorities and train the monitoring staff who work there.
   b) have to stop giving permits for the construction of factory buildings without monitoring them.
   c) have to stop monitoring the construction process of factory buildings.
   d) have to end the developments in 2018.

b) Do the following tasks in complete sentences.

1. Describe what happened in Dhaka on 24 April 2013.
2. Describe the action being taken in Dhaka in order to prevent such catastrophes in the future.
3. Outline what still has to be done in the future according to Reddy.
4. Explain why Reddy thinks that the attention given to Rana Plaza has been both good and bad for Bangladesh's garment industry.

c) Using your own words summarize the main ideas of the text. Write about 250 words.

B | Mediation

3 English – German

Read the following article from *The Guardian* about Welsh teenagers who learn to rethink racism and tell your classmates about the main aspects of the project in German.

Welsh youngsters learn to rethink racism

[…] The white men on the screen are shouting, fists jabbing the air. "Allah, Allah, who the fuck is Allah?" and "If you all hate Pakis, clap your hands". The young people watching are silent, serious. "It's embarrassing," they say afterwards. "They are making us all look bad."

The men in the film are from the *Welsh Defence League* – a spin-off of the far-right *English Defence League* – and the teenagers watching them are taking part in the *Think Project*, a three-day course aimed at stopping young white people in south Wales from getting involved in far-right extremism.

The project was created by the Swansea-based *Ethnic Youth Support Team* (EYST) in response to the racist and Islamophobic abuse experienced by the organisation's ethnic minority clients. In south Wales there were 1,421 racially motivated attacks last year. [...]

The project links with agencies working with teenagers excluded from school or young people not in work, education or training and delivers the course as part of their programmes. The material covered is wide-ranging: racism, migration, asylum, extremism, religion, human rights. [...]

"We aim to get a conversation going," explains Chris Mort, who runs the course with colleague Nicky Nijjer. "No-one listens to these kids at school. They have never had the chance to debate and have their views heard. This is about including them, never putting them down. We want to get them to be a bit more political, build them up a bit." [...]

(247 words)

Quelle: Laura Smith, *The Guardian*, 27 May 2014.

4 German – English

Sie möchten im Rahmen Ihres Austauschjahres in England einen Vortrag über Ehrenamt-Projekte für Flüchtlinge halten. Dafür haben Sie den folgenden Text auf der Homepage des *WDR* über ein besonderes Projekt in Köln gefunden. Notieren Sie die wichtigsten Fakten für Ihren Vortrag auf Englisch.

Ehrenamt-Projekt in Köln

Dass sich Deutsche für Flüchtlinge und Zuwanderer engagieren, ist ziemlich normal. Umgekehrt kommt das eher selten vor. Im Kölner Stadtbezirk Kalk helfen Zuwanderer Alteingesessenen. Und lernen so eine Menge.

Köln, Seniorenheim St. Theodor, Aufenthaltsraum: Neben einer alten Frau mit lockigem Haar sitzt Jakleen R. Die 31-Jährige liest aus einer Zeitschrift vor. [...] Seit einigen Monaten kommt sie jede Woche für zwei Stunden in das Altenheim und kümmert sich um die alten Menschen. Ehrenamtlich. [...]

„Viele Flüchtlinge und Zuwanderer wünschen sich mehr Kontakt zu – in Anführungsstrichen – echten Deutschen", erzählt Elizaveta Khan. Sie leitet das „Integrationshaus" in Kalk. „Ungefähr ein Viertel aller Teilnehmer aus jedem Kurs sind sofort zur Freiwilligenarbeit bereit." Deshalb hat der Verein vor zwei Jahren gemeinsam mit der Bürgerstiftung „*KalkGestalten*" das Ehrenamts-Projekt „Sei dabei! Für dich, für mich, für alle!" auf die Beine gestellt. Ziel ist es, Flüchtlinge zu motivieren, sich so rasch wie möglich ehrenamtlich zu betätigen. „Denn sonst gehen viele Kursteilnehmer nach den Sprachkursen wieder in ihre Familien zurück und haben keine Chance Deutsche zu treffen", meint Rainer Kreke, Sprecher der Stiftung „*KalkGestalten*". „Und so bekommen sie dann keinen Zugang zur deutschen Kultur. Die Freiwilligenarbeit kann das ändern." [...]

Der „Nebeneffekt" der Ehrenarbeit ist unbezahlbar. „Die Leute werden beim Einkaufen von ‚Deutschen' erkannt, man unterhält sich und wer weiß, was daraus erwächst. Sie haben nicht mehr das Gefühl passiv zu sein, sondern können mitgestalten und fühlen sich dadurch auf Augenhöhe. Das stärkt ihr Selbstbewusstsein", hat Elizaveta Khan beobachtet. [...]

(245 Wörter)

Quelle: Lisa von Prondzinski, 25.07.2015.

C | Production

5 Cartoon

Describe and analyze the following cartoon.

6 Diagram

Describe and analyze the following diagram.

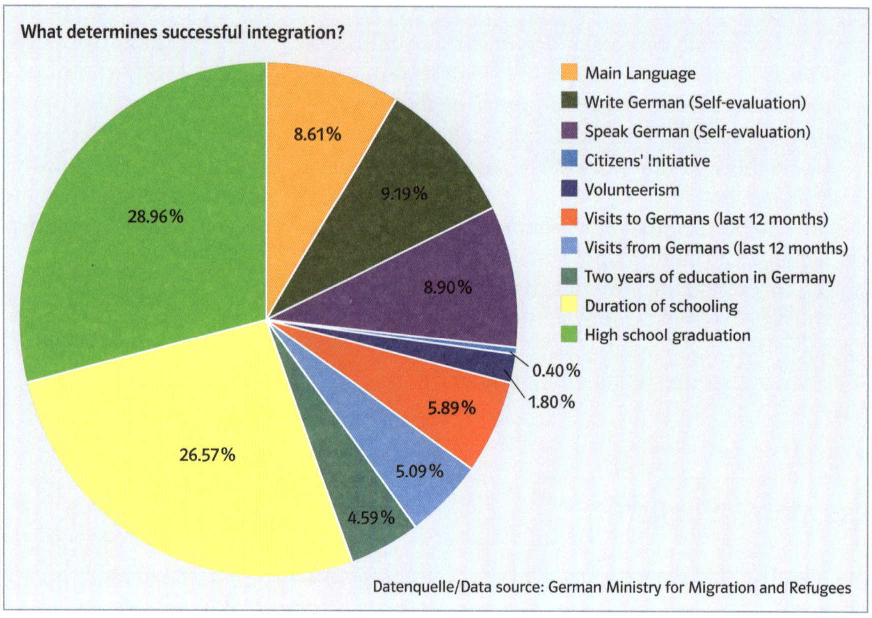

7 Composition

There is perhaps a no more widely discussed problem in Europe than that of the integration of immigrants into society. Discuss the chances and problems of integrating immigrants into society and state your point of view.

D | Business communication

8 Reminder

Write the following reminder in English.

Situation: Sie arbeiten für das deutsche Unternehmen *Maschinenbau Lutz-Lose GmbH* in Leipzig. Ihr Unternehmen hat die britische Firma *Simpsons Ideal Manufacturing* in Bristol vor zwei Monaten mit 20 CNC-Maschinen beliefert. Die vereinbarte Überweisung sollte innerhalb eines Monats geleistet werden und ist bisher nicht eingetroffen. Sie haben das britische Unternehmen bereits vor zwei Wochen an die Zahlung erinnert, aber keine Antwort erhalten. Ihre Ansprechpartnerin ist Ms Donna King, ihre E-Mail-Adresse lautet d.king@simpsons-ideal-manufacturing.com.

Aufgabe: Aufgrund des fehlenden Zahlungseingangs schreiben Sie unter Ihrem Namen und mit der E-Mail-Adresse Ihres Unternehmens (vorname.name@maschinenbau-lutz-lose.de) eine Mahnung an das britische Unternehmen.

- Verweisen Sie auf die Lieferung und die vereinbarte Zahlungsfrist.
- Senden Sie die Kopie der Rechnung Nr. B-4354 in der Anlage.
- Geben Sie dem britischen Unternehmen ein letztes Zahlungsziel von zwei Wochen vor.
- Für den Fall der Nichtzahlung weisen Sie darauf hin, dass Sie in Zukunft Ihre Zahlungsbedingungen ändern werden.
- Sie bitten um Mitteilung, falls die Rechnung in der Zwischenzeit doch schon beglichen wurde.
- Sie bieten dem britischen Unternehmen an, sich mit Ihnen in Verbindung zu setzen, falls es Fragen in Bezug auf die Zahlung gibt.
- Sie freuen sich auf den baldigen Ausgleich des Kontos.

Quellennachweis

4 iStockphoto (monkeybusinessimages), Calgary, Alberta; **5** iStockphoto (Robert Churchill), Calgary, Alberta; **9** Fotolia.com (rookie72), New York; **10** Fotolia.com (.shock), New York; **11** iStockphoto (JMichl), Calgary, Alberta; **12.1** Fotolia.com (Christopher Jones), New York; **12.2** iStockphoto (encrier), Calgary, Alberta; **14.1** iStockphoto (Maxiphoto), Calgary, Alberta; **14.2** iStockphoto (iprogressman), Calgary, Alberta; **14.3** iStockphoto (Ellica_S), Calgary, Alberta; **14.4** iStockphoto (carlopops), Calgary, Alberta; **14.5** iStockphoto (Sean2008), Calgary, Alberta; **14.6** shutterstock (Feraru Nicolae), New York, NY; **14.7** Thinkstock (Jupiterimages), München; **17.1** Fotolia.com (bertys30), New York; **17.2** shutterstock (BigLike Images), New York, NY; **17.3** shutterstock (Lucky Business), New York, NY; **17.4** shutterstock (Joana Lopes), New York, NY; **17.5** Fotolia.com (Masson), New York; **17.6** shutterstock (Supri Suharjoto), New York, NY; **17.7** shutterstock (wavebreakmedia), New York, NY; **17.8** Fotolia.com (Nathalie P), New York; **17.9** dreamstime.com (Diademimages), Brentwood, TN; **19** Fotolia.com (auremar), New York; **20.1** Fotolia.com, New York; **20.2** shutterstock (Lucky Business), New York, NY; **22** shutterstock (Thiago Leite), New York, NY; **23** iStockphoto (Lisa-Blue), Calgary, Alberta; **25** Fotolia.com (contrastwerkstatt), New York; **27.1** dreamstime.com (Maxexphoto), Brentwood, TN; **27.2** iStockphoto (Pali Rao), Calgary, Alberta; **27.3** dreamstime.com (Norman Chan), Brentwood, TN; **28** dreamstime.com (Indos82), Brentwood, TN; **29** shutterstock (Gabriel Georgescu), New York, NY; **30.1** shutterstock (Robert Kneschke), New York, NY; **30.2** Thinkstock (Creatas), München; **32** iStockphoto (Tom Nulens), Calgary, Alberta; **33** iStockphoto (sergeyryzhov), Calgary, Alberta; **36** shutterstock (Jeff Gynane), New York, NY; **37** iStockphoto (mapodile), Calgary, Alberta; **38.** shutterstock (goodluz), New York, NY; **39** shutterstock (Dikiiy), New York, NY; **40.1** www.CartoonStock.com (Chris Wildt), Bath; **40.2** www.CartoonStock.com (Chris Wildt), Bath; **41** iStockphoto (Antonio_Diaz), Calgary, Alberta; **42** iStockphoto (AlbertPego), Calgary, Alberta; **43** iStockphoto (PeopleImages), Calgary, Alberta; **44.1** Fotolia.com (Luca Oleastri), New York; **44.2** Imago (Arnulf Hettrich), Berlin; **45** Thinkstock (monkeybusinessimages), München; **46** shutterstock (wavebreakmedia), New York, NY; **47.1** shutterstock (Xerography), New York, NY; **47.2** shutterstock (Blablo101), New York, NY; **47.3** 123rf (Vitalii Zainulin), Nidderau; **47.4** shutterstock (LANTERIA), New York, NY; **47.5** shutterstock (popular.vector), New York, NY; **47.6** shutterstock (VoodooDot), New York, NY; **49** iStockphoto (Steve Debenport), Calgary, Alberta; **51** iStockphoto (Lisa Kyle Young), Calgary, Alberta; **52** iStockphoto (Hung_Chung_Chih), Calgary, Alberta; **54** shutterstock (Claudia Paulussen), New York, NY; **56** Fotolia.com (lapas77), New York; **57** Fotolia.com (alain wacquier), New York; **58.1** Imago (Lovell), Berlin; **58.2** Fotolia.com (dieter76), New York; **58.3** Ullstein Bild GmbH (Imagebroker.net), Berlin; **58.4** iStockphoto (kynny), Calgary, Alberta; **58.5** Thinkstock (iStockphoto), München; **59** iStockphoto (Yuri_Arcurs), Calgary, Alberta; **60** iStockphoto (mikkelwilliam), Calgary, Alberta; **61** iStockphoto (Yagi-Studio), Calgary, Alberta; **62** Fotolia.com (LuckyImages), New York; **64.1** iStockphoto, Calgary, Alberta; **64.2** iStockphoto (3DSculptor), Calgary, Alberta; **65** Fotolia.com (Xavier MARCHANT), New York; **66** Fotolia.com (Hendrik Schwartz), New York; **67** Thinkstock (Digital Vision/Jochen Sand), München; **68** Fotolia.com (lightpoet), New York; **69** iStockphoto (andresr), Calgary, Alberta; **71** shutterstock (Dmitry Chulov), New York, NY; **72** shutterstock (Pablo Rogat), New York, NY; **73** iStockphoto (Oko_SwanOmurphy), Calgary, Alberta; **74** iStockphoto (Fertnig), Calgary, Alberta; **75** shutterstock (FXQuadro), New York, NY; **76** Fotolia.com (Vospalej), New York; **77** iStockphoto (Peterhowell), Calgary, Alberta; **78** iStockphoto (ChristianChan), Calgary, Alberta; **80** Fotolia.com (aalutcenko), New York; **81** iStockphoto (doomko), Calgary, Alberta; **82** Fotolia.com (Francesco83), New York; **83** iStockphoto (level17), Calgary, Alberta; **87** shutterstock (racorn), New York, NY; **89** iStockphoto (Guolker), Calgary, Alberta; **91** iStockphoto (megaflopp), Calgary, Alberta; **93** Fotolia.com (Picture-Factory), New York; **94** iStockphoto (OJO_Images), Calgary, Alberta; **94** © 2015, Guardian News & Media Ltd.; **96** © 2013, Guardian News & Media Ltd.; **97** Zeit Campus; **97.1** shutterstock (Lisa Kolbasa), New York, NY; **97.2** Fotolia.com (Annatamila), New York; **97.3** shutterstock (Samo Trebizan), New York, NY; **97.4** iStockphoto (franckreporter), Calgary, Alberta; **97.5** Fotolia.com (zephyr_p), New York; **98.1** Dream Maker Software (RF), Colorado; **98.2** shutterstock (Fabio Alcini), New York, NY; **98.3** BigStockPhoto.com (hinnamsaisuy), Davis, CA; **98.4** Fotolia.com (Eskimo71), New York; **99** © 2015, Guardian News & Media Ltd.; **99** iStockphoto (manaemedia), Calgary, Alberta; **101** © 2011, Guardian News & Media Ltd.; **101** shutterstock (Pressmaster), New York, NY; **102** Quelle: n-tv.de , ppo/dpa; **102** shutterstock (mauro_grigollo), New York, NY; **103.1** iStockphoto, Calgary, Alberta; **103.2** iStockphoto (Andy Tuohy), Calgary, Alberta; **104** iStockphoto (lzf), Calgary, Alberta; **105** Copyright Guardian News & Media Ltd 2017; **106** © 2014, Guardian News & Media Ltd.; **107** Der Tagesspiegel, 10.01.2013; **108** www.CartoonStock.com (Chris Madden), Bath; **109** Fotolia.com (Syda Productions), New York; **109** © 2015, Guardian News & Media Ltd.; **111** Fotolia.com (kengmerry), New York; **111** © 2015, Guardian News & Media Ltd.; **112.1** Fotolia.com (zozzzzo), New York; **112.2** www.CartoonStock.com (Grizelda), Bath; **112** TAZ, 24.03.2012; **113** Office for National Statistics; **114** iStockphoto (Maciej Bledowski), Calgary, Alberta; **114** © 2015, Guardian News & Media Ltd.; **116** iStockphoto (Rawpixel Ltd), Calgary, Alberta; **116** © 2015, Guardian News & Media Ltd.; **117** www.CartoonStock.com (Piero Tonin), Bath; **117** WDR, 25.07.2015; **Umschlag.1** shutterstock (Maridav), New York, NY; **Umschlag.2** Thinkstock (peterfz30), München; **Lösungsheft Umschlag.1** Getty Images (Corbis Documentary), München; **Umschlag.2** Avenue Images GmbH (Westend61), Hamburg.

Sollte es in einem Einzelfall nicht gelungen sein, den korrekten Rechteinhaber ausfindig zu machen, so werden berechtigte Ansprüche selbstverständlich im Rahmen der üblichen Regelungen abgegolten.